The Final Trumpet

How Prophecy Foretold The World's History Exactly

by

R. W. Mills

authorHOUSE™

1663 LIBERTY DRIVE, SUITE 200
BLOOMINGTON, INDIANA 47403
(800) 839-8640
WWW.AUTHORHOUSE.COM

© 2005 R. W. Mills. All Rights Reserved.

No part of this book may be reproduced, stored in a retrieval system, or transmitted by any means without the written permission of the author.

First published by AuthorHouse 03/01/05

ISBN: 1-4208-1270-X (e)
ISBN: 1-4208-1269-6 (sc)
ISBN: 1-4208-1268-8 (dj)

Library of Congress Control Number: 2004099140

Printed in the United States of America
Bloomington, Indiana

This book is printed on acid-free paper.

TABLE OF CONTENTS

FOREWORD ix
INTRODUCTION xi
WHY STUDY PROPHECY? xii
BIBLICAL PROPHECIES 1
THE 70 WEEK PROPHECY 7
TWO QUESTIONS 14
DECEIVERS ARE COMING 15
WARS & RUMORS OF WAR ARE COMING 15
FAMINES AND EARTHQUAKES ARE COMING 16
PERSECUTION & DEATH ARE COMING 16
GOSPEL PREACHED TO WHOLE WORLD 16
ABOMINATION OF DESOLATION TIME TO FLEE 17
THE GREAT TRIBULATION 18
ONE GENERATION 20
FALSE PROPHETS ARE COMING 20
NIGHT FALLS ON THE JEWS 21
THE DAY AND HOUR UNKNOWN 22
REVELATION 1:1-3 Prologue 28
DATING WRITING OF REVELATION 29
REVELATION 1:4-8 Greetings and Doxology 30
REVELATION 1:9-18 31
REVELATION 1:19 OUTLINE FOR BOOK 32
REVELATION 2: 1-7 To the Church in Ephesus 33
REVELATION 2:8-11 To the Church in Smyrna 34

REVELATION 2:12-17 To the Church in Pergamum 35

REVELATION 2:18-29 To the Church in Thyatira 36

REVELATION 3:1-6 To the Church in Sardis 37

REVELATION 3:7-13 To the Church in Philadelphia 38

REVELATION 3:14-22 To the Church in Laodicea 39

CHRIST STANDS AT THE DOOR 40

REVELATION 4 The Throne in Heaven 41

REVELATION 5 The Enthronement Of Christ 42

REVELATION 6 The Seals 43

REVELATION 7:1-8 SEALING THE 144,000 51

REVELATION 7:9-17 The Great Multitude in White Robes 52

REVELATION 8:1-5 The Seventh Seal and the Golden Censer 54

2 THESSALONIANS 2:1-12 The Man of Lawlessness 55

REVELATION 8:6 The Seven Trumpets 57

REVELATION 8:7 The 1st Trumpet 58

REVELATION 8:8-9 The 2nd Trumpet 60

REVELATION 8:10-11 The 3rd Trumpet 61

REVELATION 8:11-13 The 4th Trumpet 62

REVELATION 9:1-12 The 5th Trumpet (1st Woe) 63

REVELATION 9:13-21 The 6th Trumpet (2nd Woe) 66

THE REVIVED ROMAN POWER 68

REVELATION 10 The Angel and the Little Scroll [Book] 69

REVELATION 11:1-14 The Two Witnesses 72

REVELATION 11:15-19 The Seventh Trumpet 76

QUICK REVIEW 77

REVELATION 12 The Woman and the Dragon 80

REVELATION 13:1-12 The Beast out of the Sea	82
DANIEL 7:15-28 The Interpretation of the Dream	83
REVELATION 13:11-18 The Beast out of the Earth	87
REVELATION 14:1-5 The Lamb and the 144,000	90
REVELATION 14:6-13 The Three Angels	90
REVELATION 14:14-20 The Harvest of the Earth	92
REVELATION 15 Seven Angles With Seven Pkagues	93
REVELATION 16 The Seven Bowls of God's Wrath	94
REVELATION 17 The Woman on the Beast	104
REVELATION 18 The Fall of Babylon	107
REVELATION 19:1-10 The Wedding of the Lamb	109
REVELATION 19:11-16 KING OF KINGS	110
REVELATION 20:1-6 Two Expansions & Satan's Demise	111
REVELATION 21 The New Jerusalem	115
REVELATION 22	118
THE FINAL WARNING	120
QUICK REVIEW	121
THE END OF TIME	126
COMPLETE REVIEW OF TRIBULATION	133
ANTICHRIST OR ANTICHRISTS	138
FINAL REVIEW	141
CONCLUSION	149
GETTING READY	151
THE TEN COMMANDMENTS	152
BONDAGE BOYS	154
WHAT DO I NEED TO DO?	155

HURDLES	155
RECOMMEMDED READING	159
THE FIRST BOWL	95
THE SECOND BOWL	96
THE THIRD BOWL	97
THE FOURTH BOWL	97
THE FIFTH BOWL	98
THE SIXTH BOWL	99
THE SIXTH BOWL	100
THE SEVENTH BOWL	101

FOREWORD

This book, ***The Final Trumpet*** was created as a result of writing ***Truth-Not Exactly***. Many who read ***Truth-Not Exactly*** requested as to the possibility of creating a stand-alone book covering Revelation. ***The Final Trumpet*** is that book with additional teaching, reviews, and visual aids. It contains little speculation, since it is based on doing a survey of history - especially the Christian Church's history, and then matching history to the prophecy. The book of Revelation, I believe, contains God's foreknowledge in written form given to the Church for our benefit. Recorded history is the fulfillment of God's foreknowledge. God, who wrote Revelation, is the same one who controls all history. The assumption is that history would match sequentially the predicted events that are revealed sequentially in Revelation. I know that truth, when clearly explained and then understood, can be used by the Holy Spirit to change lives.

This book is for one purpose. It is designed to show that the God of the Bible has a master plan that He has been executing on schedule since the beginning of this world. ***The Final Trumpet*** is about the next major event in history. This event is the return of Christ at the Final Trumpet. I know that a book is an excellent tool for leading people to Christ. I gave my youngest brother a book on prophecy in May of 1980. After he had read it, he came to me with a series of questions and concerns about his future and eternity. The day after participating in the miracle of my first daughter's birth, I had the opportunity on June 20, 1980, to present the Gospel to my brother and watch him accept Christ. As a new Christian, my brother was the first person that I had the honor of helping into the kingdom of God. I have dedicated this book to him.

Each person is born into this world in a family or situation where someone is going to influence what values, beliefs, prejudices, world-view and theological understanding one acquires. The question is always the same. Is it based on Truth? Both my youngest brother and myself were not taught anything about God, Christ, Christianity, and/or the Bible. We developed our world-view from parents, teachers, books, friends, and the ever-influencing television. We saw religion and assumed it was for the uniformed and weak. I believe everyone asks themselves sometime during their life what is the Truth.

This book is about a coming event that is going to happen as surely as the sun will rise tomorrow. It is an event for which one wants to be prepared. This book will cause any reader to assess today their potential place in eternity. It is not important what I believe is true. It is only important what is true. There is a God, who has revealed in Revelation exactly what did come to pass for the last two thousand years. This may cause one to stop and think about the next event that God has told us will take pass in the near future. At this event there are no second chances. If the Final Trumpet sounds and you have not made a conscious decision to choose truth, then God reveals a fate that no one would want. This book may have been a gift. Thank that person, even if you ultimately disagree, for they did it out of concern about your future well-being.

When God moved me to write **Truth-Not Exactly,** I resisted. I had two reasons that I shared in my first book: I am not a writer and the other was fear. God reminded me who my Aaron was. Neither book would have been published without the loving support of my dear wife. God has kept His word when His small still voice spoke to me and said, "She will be more than you can imagine." She is all that God promised and more than this man deserves. She has been my partner in ministry for almost thirty years. For that, I am thankful and acknowledge her assistance with the writing of these books.

INTRODUCTION

I was raised as an Atheist, who went searching for God as detailed in the book *Truth-Not Exactly*. The scientific laws of this universe, combined with deductive logic, demanded a first cause or Creator. Logic dictated that this Creator would not create without purpose. Furthermore, I derived that He may have communicated with us. I went on a search for Revealed Truth that contained information they –the writers - were unable to know as truth at that time. Many examples were found and are in *Truth-Not Exactly*. This led to a review of prophecy in the Bible. Fortunately, the Greeks translated the Bible into Greek about 285 B.C. This meant the Jews or Christians would not be able to make Prophecy after the fact. I discovered so many detailed fulfilled prophecies that it challenged my entire upbringing and mindset. I knew men could not predict the future such as was found in the Bible. I came to the conclusion that the Bible was divine with the Seal of God on it. I had to agree with what Isaiah said thousands of years ago.

In Isaiah 41:23, the prophet hurled out the ultimate challenge to the heathen gods, **"Show the things that are to come here after, that we may know that ye are gods."** Being in the 21st Century, it appears that the same questions or challenges were asked over three thousand years ago. **If you can tell the future then it would prove that you are a God.** If the Bible has prophecy that predicts future events exactly, then this is the **seal of God** that separates the Bible from all other non-divine books. Who can predict the rise and fall of empires, the way future battles will be fought along with their outcomes, and what cities or races will survive or become extinct? No human can do such a thing. The prophets of God, who spoke and wrote for God, have shown the mark of divine help.

During the end of the 20th Century, Christianity became extremely focused on prophecy and the ever-changing end-time scenarios that were tied to daily events found in the news. When I became a Christian, I had an entirely new vocabulary to learn. Many of the words came with multiple definitions and interpretations. To say the least, I was a bit confused by words like Rapture, Antichrist, The Beast of the Sea, The Beast of the Earth, Two Witnesses, The Great Tribulation, 144,000, Mark of the Beast, The Four Horseman, The Seven Trumpets, The Seven Seals, etc. I just wanted to understand the truth.

WHY STUDY PROPHECY?

This was a question that I received every year from my students as we began to study the prophecy of the Bible. People want to know the future. The world since the end of World War II, has experienced a rebirth of interest in astrology and fortune telling. Science may be our God, but we will turn to voodoo if we think we can peer down the road and know what is coming. Millions consult their horoscopes daily in over a thousand newspapers nationwide. There are countless fulltime and part time astrologers and foretellers in America alone. All promise to be able to tell us the future.

We have become overwhelmed by the largeness, pace, and complexities of this world. It is understandable to look for help. The problem with seeking help in these places is that these are forms of "fatalism." People want to know what will happen to them more often to escape responsibility. "I know the future and I cannot change it." G.K. Chesterton has said, "When a man ceases to believe in nothing, he will believe anything." Some even believe poor advice from another person who can supposedly tell your future based upon the position of the stars that lock your destiny. In any event, they remove your right to choose if you give them credence. Just before WWII, Archibald MacLiesh penned, "The generation to which I belong believes…in a predetermined pattern of life and they prophesy because their fate is sealed. Our generation has fled to fate," he explains, "not by opposing it, but by searching it out in order that we might yield to it, and by yielding then not only our responsibilities but our will."

The Christian can fall into fatalism. When one believes the church has the power to be victorious and it is the will of God they will act differently. The result of such thinking during the second great awakening caused the establishment of Bible societies, home missions, and world-wide missionary movements. What is the expectation of the 21st Century church and Christians today about the future? It will be tied to what we believe prophecy says. If we believe that we are sliding into a moral decline, then it is easy to fall into the trap of fatalism. Remember, prophecy is not merely prediction, it is judgment and it is promise. The biblical view is that what God does is always vitally related to what man does. We will look at Scripture to see what God has said about our future as believers and the role and expectation for His church.

BIBLICAL PROPHECIES

Who can predict the future? We humans with all of our collective genius are unable to predict future events and trends. To know advanced information is the privilege of the Divine only.

In I Kings 14:15-16, the following prophecy was given:

> "And the Lord will strike Israel, so that it will be like a reed swaying in the water. He will uproot Israel from this good land that he gave to their forefathers and scatter them beyond the River, because they provoked the Lord to anger by making Asherah poles. And he will give Israel up because of the sins Jeroboam has committed and caused Israel to commit."

This prophecy was given in 910 B.C. Predicting the destruction of a nation was not high risk as it was a common occurrence in those times. What makes this interesting is where the captives would be taken. The river is the Euphrates and the conquerors are the Assyrians, who rose up in 722 B.C. and destroyed the Northern Kingdom and carried thousands north across the Euphrates. Assyrian records indicate that Sargon captured the Northern Kingdom. A record has been found in the ruins of Sargon's palace that he carried away 27,290 Israelite captives.

The next set of prophecies added a specific time period for the end of one Empire, predicted the leader who would win, and predicted an extremely unique ending for Israel. Isaiah prophesied the following in 1475 B.C:

> "Then Isaiah said to Hezekiah, 'Hear the word of the Lord Almighty: The time will surely come when everything in your palace, and all that your fathers have stored up until this day, will be carried off to Babylon. Nothing will be left,' says the Lord. 'And some of your descendants, your flesh and blood who will be taken away, and they will become eunuchs in the palace of the king of Babylon"[1] Isaiah 39:5-7.

In 606-605 B.C., Babylon attacked Israel. Then Jeremiah stated Israel would be held captive for 70 years in 600 B.C. This was a final warning. Jeremiah 25:9-12:

---

[1] Eunuch, a castrated man in charge of a harem of women.

"I will summon all the peoples of the north and my servant Nebuchadnezzar king of Babylon, declares the Lord, and I will bring them against this land and its inhabitants and against all the surrounding nations.....This whole country will become a desolate wasteland, and these nations will serve the king of Babylon seventy years. But when the seventy years are fulfilled, I will punish the king of Babylon and his nation, the land of the Babylonians, for their guilt, declares the Lord, and it will be desolate forever."

Did this happen? Total destruction – the city of Jerusalem and the Temple were completely decimated. The Jews are now in Babylon for 70 years.

DANIEL INTERPRETS THE KING OF BABYLON'S DREAM

This prophecy is found in Daniel 2:24-45: "Then Daniel went to Arioch, whom the king had appointed to execute the wise men of Babylon, and said to him, "Do not execute the wise men of Babylon. Take me to the king, and I will interpret his dream for him." Arioch took Daniel to the king at once and said, "I have found a man among the exiles from Judah who can tell the king what his dream means." The king asked Daniel (also called Belteshazzar), "Are you able to tell me what I saw in my dream and interpret it?" Daniel replied, "No wise man, enchanter, magician or diviner can explain to the king the mystery he has asked about, but there is a God in heaven who reveals mysteries. He has shown King Nebuchadnezzar what will happen in days to come. Your dream and the visions that passed through your mind as you lay on your bed are these: "As you were lying there, O king, your mind turned to things to come, and the revealer of mysteries showed you what is going to happen. As for me, this mystery has been revealed to me, not because I have greater wisdom than other living men, but so that you, O king, may know the interpretation and that you may understand what went through your mind. "You looked, O king, and there before you stood a large statue—an enormous, dazzling statue, awesome in appearance. The head of the statue was made of pure gold, its chest and arms of silver, its belly and thighs of bronze, its legs of iron, its feet partly of iron and partly of baked clay. While you were watching, a rock was cut out, but not by human hands. It struck the statue on its feet of iron and clay and smashed them. Then the iron, the clay, the bronze, the silver and the gold were broken to pieces at the same time and became like chaff on a threshing floor in the summer. The wind swept them away without leaving a trace. But the rock that struck the statue became a huge mountain and filled the whole earth. "This was the dream, and now we will interpret it to the king. You, O king, are the king of kings. The God of heaven has given you dominion and power and might and glory; in your hands he has placed mankind and the beasts of the field and the birds of the air. Wherever they live, he has made you ruler over them all. You are that head of gold. "After you, another kingdom will rise, inferior to yours. Next, a third kingdom, one of bronze, will rule over the whole earth. Finally, there will be a fourth kingdom, strong as iron—for iron breaks and smashes everything—and as iron breaks things to pieces, so it will crush and break all the others. Just as you saw that the feet and toes were partly of baked clay and partly of iron, so this will be a divided kingdom; yet it will have some of the strength of iron in it, even as you saw iron mixed with clay. As the toes were partly iron and partly clay, so this kingdom will be partly strong and partly brittle. And just as you saw the iron mixed with baked clay, so the people will be a mixture and will not remain united, any more than iron mixes with clay. "In the time of those kings, the God of heaven will set up a kingdom that will never be destroyed, nor will it be left to another people. It will crush all those kingdoms and bring them to an end, but it will itself endure forever. This is the meaning of the vision of the rock cut out of a mountain, but not by human hands—a rock that broke the iron, the bronze, the clay, the silver and the gold to pieces. "The great God has shown the king what will take place in the future. The dream is true and the interpretation is trustworthy.""

Here Daniel describes the four kingdoms and the coming Kingdom of God.

Another of God's prophets, Isaiah; also predicted that Cyrus would come and defeat Babylon and free the Israelites and unbelievably allow Israel to return to Jerusalem. Isaiah 45:13 states:

"I will raise up Cyrus in my righteousness; I will make all his ways straight. He will rebuild my city and set my exiles free, but not for a price or reward, says the Lord Almighty."

What transpired was incredible and highly unpredictable. One hundred and fifty years prior to his birth the prophets recorded that Cyrus who was not yet born, would set them free. He is mentioned a total of twenty-three times in the Old Testament. It is Cyrus who overthrew the Babylonian Empire on the night that the famous and mysterious "handwriting on the wall" appeared. Babylon was considered impregnable. According to historians such as Herodotus, Rawlinson, and Prideaux, a sixty-mile wall estimated to be over two hundred feet high and eighty-seven feet thick enclosed the city of Babylon. Babylon had a moat of equal width. Passing through the center of Babylon was the Euphrates River. Babylon figured that, with its water supply and gardens, Cyrus would be wasting his time with the siege of Babylon. In fact, the Babylonians were celebrating their festival as usual.

Cyrus discovered when this festival would happen and decided this would be the time to strike, since the Babylonians would be in a spirit of revelry and drunkenness. Cyrus diverted the water from the Euphrates with a dam to temporarily dry the Euphrates riverbed. He marched his armies into the city in surprise and quickly defeated the Babylonian Empire. The interior river gates had been left open along the river due to the celebrations. Cyrus was successful in bringing down Babylon in 537 B.C. Cyrus was shown the prophecies concerning him in the Holy Scriptures. It detailed how he would win the battle over the Babylonians, how the river would be dry and the gates would be opened before him. The scrolls that were shown to him revealed that he would conquer many more nations. Cyrus defeated a total of fourteen nations as predicted. To confirm the additional prophecy as to the length of captivity being seventy years, this meant it must conclude in 536 B.C. at which time Cyrus needed to release his new slaves. Land, treasure, and slaves were what victors collected as they built their empires. Cyrus did something that defied all logic. In 536 B.C., Cyrus issued a decree in writing simply giving Israel permission to return. He also did exactly as predicted and asked for no price.

As you have read, Daniel explained to Nebuchadnezzar concerning the interpretation of his dream: "You are the ruler over all and are the Head of Gold. After you another kingdom will rise, however it will be inferior to yours since it is represented by silver." History tells us the Medo-Persian Empire did conquer Babylon. Daniel is given a dream that makes identification easier. In Chapter 7:2-14; "Daniel spake and said, I saw in my vision by night, and, behold, the four winds of the heaven strove upon the great sea. And four great beasts came up from the sea, diverse one from another. The first was like a lion, and had eagle's wings: I beheld till the wings thereof were plucked, and it was lifted up from the earth, and made stand upon the feet as a man, and a man's heart was given to it. And up itself on one side, and it had three ribs in the mouth of it between the teeth of it: and they said thus unto it, Arise, devour much flesh. After this I beheld, and lo another, like a leopard, which had upon the back of it four wings of a fowl; the beast had also four heads; and dominion was given to it. After this I saw in the night visions, and behold a fourth beast, dreadful and terrible, and strong exceedingly; and it had great iron teeth: it devoured and brake in pieces, and stamped the residue with the feet of it: and it was diverse from all the beasts that were before it; and it had ten horns."

A lion, the symbol of royal power for Babylon, represented the first empire. The second beast is bear-like with three ribs in his mouth and "raised up on one side." This referred to the fact that Persia dominated Media. The three ribs are the three major conquests – Babylon, Lydia, and Egypt. The third empire looked like a leopard and on its back had four wings like a bird. The leopard is a powerful and swift animal. The next Empire represents Alexander the Great with his rapid conquests. It was so quick that at age thirty-two, it is said that Alexander had conquered the world and wept because there were no more worlds to conquer. History recorded that the Grecian empire was divided into four parts, as prophecy said at Alexander's death. Each of Alexander's generals received a piece of the empire. Lysimachus received Thrace and Bithynia, Cassander controlled Greece and Macedon, Seleucus ruled Babylonia and Syria, and Ptolemy governed Palestine, Egypt, and Arabia. The fourth kingdom was the Roman Empire. It had iron teeth and would crush and devour its victims and trample underfoot whatever was left. It was different from the other beasts, and it had ten horns. Rome did separate into ten nations as predicted. Daniel 2:44 predicted that during the time of this empire a new empire would be established that would never be destroyed. This clearly commits to a time when the coming "Kingdom of God" is to be established. This prophecy states that the Messiah would come when the Roman Empire was in existence. In 63 B.C., Rome conquered Palestine. The Bible and history does record that the Kingdom of God, along with Jesus the Messiah, did enter history during Rome's reign of power as predicted.

This seemed impossible, that these prophesies about the rising and falling of empires would actually happen as predicted. This went against everything I had been indoctrinated to believe. My education did not allow for miracles and supposed fulfillment of prophecies. Even the Church of the last two centuries was teaching that miracles do not happen and that the prophecies were recorded after their fulfillment was met.

This would have been possible to accept: that maybe the Jews recorded these events after their occurrences except for one simple problem, the Old Testament was translated into the Greek language (Septuagint) about 285 B.C. This means that all fulfilled prophecy after that date could be guaranteed to have been written prior to its fulfillment. The Greeks did for me what the Hebrews could not. **They provided certainty that God was in control and His prophecies were true!**

> **Key point:** 19th & 20th Century liberal theologians of the Christian church have been indoctrinating the masses in America's Society by stating that miracles do not exist and that predicting the future is not possible even if the Bible states it clearly. Today's theologians spend their time making assumptions and arguing whether a book, a verse, etc. was written 900 B.C. or 910 B.C. or whether it is in the correct textual style for that period of history. They state that there is no other written support to collaborate the Bible, then it cannot be trusted. Liberal theologians with their higher criticism of the Bible miss the point. Ezra sealed the Old Testament around 400 B.C. and the Greeks ordered that the Hebrew Old Testament be translated into their language well before 250 B.C.
>
> **Question:** Why would Greece allow the Hebrew Old Testament to be translated? It clearly states that the Grecian Empire would fall and which nation would be the next Empire to rise. Today, we in the 21st Century with our computers and all our financial models are still unable to predict whether the stock market will go up or down next week. As an atheist, even I was getting the point. The Bible had hundreds of fulfilled prophecies each guaranteed to have been written hundreds of years prior to the fulfillments by the Grecian Empire. Alexander The Great, after conquering the Jews, was shown that God had chosen him. The Jews also showed him what other nations would fall before him. Those nations did fall as predicted.

Daniel 2:24-45 unbelievably predicted the four successive empires as follows: Babylon, Medo-Persian (also known as Assyrian), Greek, and Roman. It showed that the Roman Empire would last the longest and would have some kind of split as represented by the legs of the image. History does tell us that Rome did split into eastern and western divisions, with capitals at Rome and Constantinople. Daniel reveals that the Kingdom of God would be set up during the time of Rome. Daniel has so many prophecies with such detail that the critics insist that, since they are so exact, they have to been written after the fact. Let's move on quickly to one of the most important and least understood prophecies in the Bible, known as the Seventy Weeks. Most start with their conclusions and force Scripture to fit their personal bias that they have received, either growing up in their church, attending Bible school, or reading one of the mass produced and highly popular books on prophecy during the end of the 20th Century.

> **RECORDED HISTORICAL EVENTS DURING THE PERIOD KNOWN AS THE SEVENTY WEEKS PROPHECY**
>
> The time period covered by the Seventy Weeks prophecy is as follows:
> 457 B.C. Artaxerxes I issues decree to Ezra to rebuild city and walls
> 408 B.C. Jews rebuilt the walls of Jerusalem and re-established their
> civil and religious systems in forty-nine years
> 334 B.C. Alexander the Great invades Asia
> 285 B.C. Translation of Septuagint Version as commanded by Ptolemy Philadelphus
> 63 B.C. Julius Caesar officially recognized as the Pontifex Maximus
> 35 B.'C Battle of Actium Rome is victorious
> 4 B.C. Birth of Christ
> 26 A.D. Beginning of Christ's earthly ministry
> 30 A.D. Christ is crucified
> 34 A.D. Philip went to Samaria and preached Christ to them

The dates given here are historical facts and they will not have their full meaning and impact until they can be tied into what God has revealed. Once God's plan and purpose are understood, then the seventy-week prophecy comes alive as fulfilled prophecy. We will begin by actually reading the prophecies without any interpretations.

THE 70 WEEK PROPHECY

We are using the New International Version (NIV). This is something that is very helpful in getting to see what is meant. Both are correct translations. If you are unfamiliar, as I was initially, then having a Bible with multiple versions along with a Bible commentary helps to put verses in their proper relationship to other Scripture and its correct historical context.

Daniel 9:24 "Seventy weeks [of years, or 490 years] are decreed upon your people and upon your holy city [Jerusalem], to finish and put an end to transgression, to seal up and make full the measure of sin, to purge away and make expiation and reconciliation for sin, to bring in everlasting righteousness (permanent moral and spiritual rectitude in every area and relation) to seal up vision and prophecy and prophet, and to anoint a Holy of Holies." **The Holy Bible, NIV**

Daniel 9:25 "Know therefore and understand that from the going forth of the commandment to restore and to build Jerusalem until [the coming of] the Anointed One, a Prince, shall be seven weeks [of years] and sixty-two weeks [of years]; it shall be built again with [city] square and moat, but in troublous times." **The Holy Bible, NIV**

Daniel 9:26 "After the 62 'weeks,' the Anointed King will be cut off. His followers will desert him. And everything he has will be taken away from him. The army of the ruler who will come will destroy the city and the temple. The end will come like a flood. War will continue until the end. The LORD has ordered that many places be destroyed." **NIV**

Daniel 9:27 "A covenant will be put into effect with many people for one 'week.' In the middle of the 'week' sacrifices and offerings will come to an end. In one part of the temple a hated thing that destroys will be set up. It will remain until the LORD brings the end he has ordered." **NIV**

The day for year rule in Scripture is used throughout the Bible and it is usually obvious as to when the rule applies. Bible scholars are concerned with making sure we know what the text meant. We, as lay people, primarily want to know what it means in simple terms. The concept and process is a very common sense approach. The first part of the process is called *Exegesis*. The goal is to find out what the text originally meant – what was the writer saying, to whom, and in what context. The second part of the process is called *Hermeneutics.*

Hermeneutics is learning to hear that same meaning in the context of our day. It involves the application, or incorporation, of truth into our lives. The secret of finding truth is in learning to ask the right questions.

Let's begin to dissect Daniel 9:24-27

Daniel 9:24

The Lord has appointed 70 Weeks for your people and your city. This means 7 X 70 = 490 Years, the total years of this prophecy.

1. To finish the transgression
2. To make an end of sins
3. To make reconciliation for iniquity
4. To bring everlasting righteousness
5. To seal up the vision and prophecy
6. To anoint the most Holy

The Anointed One will accomplish Items 1-6. I will explain in detail what is meant by these important tasks, especially in light of being able to

The Final Trumpet

identify who was the Messiah. This prophecy tells us when he was to appear. This is critical.

Daniel 9:25

1. There will be a seven-week period. (7 X 7 = 49 Years)
2. Then there will be a sixty-two week period. (7 X 62 = 434 Years)
3. The first seven-week period begins when the decree to rebuild Jerusalem is given.
4. At the end of the sixty-two weeks, the Anointed King will come to Jerusalem. The anointed one, or Messiah, will be made known at the end of sixty-nine weeks or 483 Years.
5. It will be done in times of trouble.

Daniel 9:26

1. Sometime after the sixty-two week period is over, the Anointed King is cut off. This means sometime during the seventh week.
2. His followers desert him. These followers would be called His disciples.
3. Everything is taken away from the Anointed King.
4. The army of the ruler will come and destroy the city and temple. This states that the Empire in control will destroy Jerusalem and the Temple.
5. The end comes like a flood and there is war right up until the end.
6. Many places will be destroyed – more than Jerusalem will be destroyed.

Daniel 9:27

1. A covenant will be put in place for one week – that totals 70.
2. In the middle of that week (3-½ years), sacrifices and offerings will come to an end.
3. He shall cause the sacrifice and the obligation to cease.

The following events happened in accordance with Daniel 9:24-27: Jerusalem was to be restored. The Messiah was to arrive 483 years after the command to rebuild. The rebuilding is fully documented by Ezra as a time of trouble, just as predicted, and the city was completed in the required forty-nine years. Nehemiah did have hindrances up until the completion in 409 B.C. Nehemiah 4:7-8, "But when Sanballat, Tobiah, the Arabs, the

Ammonites, and the men of Ashdod heard that the repairs to Jerusalem's walls had gone ahead and that the gaps were being closed, they were very angry. They all plotted together to come and fight against Jerusalem and stir up trouble against it." It took Nehemiah and company fifty-two days to build the walls. It took a total of forty-nine years under the administrations of Ezra and Nehemiah to restore the sacred constitutions and civil establishment of the Jews.

History records that Christ was crucified in April, 30 A.D. His ministry started three and one-half years prior to being cutoff in the midst of the last week, this means that John the Baptist would have baptized Jesus Christ in late 26 A.D. officially starting His ministry. Daniel 9:24 stated that God Anointed the Most Holy. Matthew 3:16-17, "As soon as Jesus was baptized, he went up out of the water. At that moment, heaven was opened and he saw the Spirit of God descend like a dove and light on him. And a voice from heaven said, 'This is my Son, whom I love; with him I am well pleased.'"

God identified Jesus as the Most Holy One, fulfilling the prophecy above. This meant that counting backwards 483 years would bring us to the 457 B.C date, which was when Artaxerxes I decreed the Jews to rebuild their city and walls.

Some Bible critics would like the date to start the 70th week prophecy as the date Cyrus released the Jews in 536 B.C. or another of Artaxerxes I decrees in 444 B.C. Each position has its defenders and reasons. However, once you know who the Anointed One is and the time of His death, then a historical fact drives the starting point of the Seventy Weeks Prophecy. The Jews were quite aware of the expected arrival time of the Messiah. The three wise men, or kings, of the east knew when Jesus was to be born. John the Baptist knew when He was due. Herod knew and tried to stop it. It was 26 A.D. and counting back 483 years is 457 B.C. timeframe. In 457 B.C., Artaxerxes I did issue a specific decree, which clearly included rebuilding Jerusalem and its walls.

Higher criticism and liberal theologians dismissed the concept that Cyrus, or any king, would release slaves for free. However, archeological evidence has been found that confirms what is in Scripture – slaves released for free. The Cyrus Cylinder, as it is known, details the battle and the eventual release of the Jews. This cylinder is now in the British Museum in London for all to see. Again, the critics of the Bible are wrong, but never silenced. Marketing gurus know if you repeat something long enough and loud enough, most unwarily accept it as truth only because they have heard it over and over. Liberal theologians obviously understand this marketing ploy.

ANOINTED ONE MUST FULFILL, IF TRULY THE MESSIAH

April, 30 A.D. (3½ years after Jesus' baptism) would be the cutting off of the Anointed One (Messiah). This is an historical fact. Jesus was crucified in 30 A.D. Jesus would have to fulfill the list below from Daniel 9:24-27 if He was really the Messiah:

To finish the transgression
To make an end of sins
To make reconciliation for iniquity
To bring everlasting righteousness
To seal up the vision and prophecy
In the middle of that week, sacrifices and offerings will come to an end
At three and one-half, there is a change in sacrifices
He shall cause the sacrifice and the obligation to cease

First, we need to provide a little background information. Second, we will explain what this meant. God's Old Testament covenant was based on laws and the keeping of laws. God chose the Jews for a purpose and it was to bless all mankind. They were given specific instructions concerning their relationship to God. They had prophets who were sent at various times to give the Jews warnings when they veered off track. God had established a temporary atonement for sin by having the high priest once a year make a sacrifice of an unblemished lamb on the altar in the Holy of Holies in the temple in Jerusalem. What I found interesting was that they tied a rope around the High Priest's waist in case he died after he entered the Holy of Holies. If the High Priest had not asked forgiveness for all his sins, or had some secret sin, then he would be struck down. Since only the High Priest was allowed to enter the Holy of Holies, the rope was their only way of retrieval should something happen to him.

Jesus was known as the Lamb of God, The Holy One. When John came baptizing, Luke 3:15-16 states, "The people were waiting. They were expecting something. They were all wondering in their hearts if John might be the Christ. John answered them all, I baptize you with water. But One who is more powerful than I am will come. I'm not good enough to untie the straps of his sandals. He will baptize you with the Holy Spirit and with fire." All the world was anticipating the coming of an Anointed One who was Holy.

He was to **"FINISH THE TRANSGRESSION"** once and for all. He became sin for us. No future sacrifice is needed, it was finished at the cross. As Jesus was dying, he cried "IT IS FINISHED."

He was **"TO MAKE AN END OF SINS."** John announced "Look! The Lamb of God! He takes away the sin of the world" (John 1:29). Jesus ended the old system of sacrifices. Jesus paid for all sin – past, present, and future. It was done.

He was **"TO MAKE RECONCILIATION FOR INEQUITY."** Reconciliation here means the same as it does the many times it is used in Leviticus. It was rendered "**to make atonement**." Hebrews 2:17 states, "For this reason he had to be made like his brothers in every way, in order that he might become a merciful and faithful high priest in service to God, and that he might **make atonement** for the sins of the people" (Holy Bible NIV). Colossians 1:20-22 clearly states that we are reconciled, "and through him to **reconcile** to himself all things, whether things on earth or things in heaven, by making peace through his blood, shed on the cross. Once you were alienated from God and were enemies in your minds because of your evil behavior. But now **he has reconciled** you by Christ's physical body through death to present you **holy in his sight, without blemish and free from accusation.**" Note we are free from accusation – we are reconciled back to God by the redemptive work of the Anointed One.

He was **"TO BRING IN EVERLASTING RIGHTEOUSNESS."** Jesus, the Anointed One, accomplished this. Romans 5:17-21 boldly declares that we have been made righteous by the Anointed One: "For if because of one man's trespass (lapse, offense) death reigned through that one, much more surely will those who receive [God's] overflowing grace (unmerited favor) and the free gift of righteousness (putting them into right standing with Himself) reign as kings in life through the one Man Jesus Christ (the Messiah, the Anointed One). As one man's trespass (one man's false step and falling away) led to condemnation for all men, **so one Man's act of righteousness** leads to **acquittal *and* right standing with God and life for all men**. For just as by one man's disobedience (failing to hear, heedlessness, and carelessness) the many were constituted sinners. So, by one Man's obedience the many will be **constituted righteous (made acceptable to God**, brought into right standing with Him). But then Law came in, [only] to expand *and* increase the trespass [making it more apparent]. But where sin increased *and* abounded, grace (God's unmerited favor) has surpassed it *and* increased the more *and* superabounded, So that, [just] as sin has reigned in death, [so] grace (His unearned and undeserved favor) might reign also through **righteousness (right standing with God)** which issues in eternal life through Jesus Christ (the Messiah, the Anointed One) our Lord" Holy Bible NIV. The New Testament is full of what is known as the NEW COVENANT, a better covenant, one that fulfilled and superceded the law and the Old Testament.

He was **"TO SEAL UP VISION AND PROPHECY."** To seal is derived from the ancient custom of attaching a seal to a document to show that it was genuine. Christ "sealed" Old Testament prophecy by fulfilling what was written of him. Acts 3:18 says, "Thus has **God fulfilled what He foretold by the mouth of all the prophets**, that His Christ (the Messiah) should undergo ill treatment *and* be afflicted *and* suffer." Jesus is the fulfillment of the Old Testament prophets and vision. This was fully explained with examples in *Truth-Not Exactly.*

"HE SHALL CAUSE THE SACRIFICE AND THE OBLIGATION TO CEASE." The old sacrifice (a type, or forerunner) had to be repeated. With the perfect sacrifice, THE LAMB OF GOD, sin was completely paid for. It did happen at three-and-one-half years, or in the middle of the seventh week. Jesus was cut off and crucified in the middle of the seventieth week as prophesied. God's requirement was satisfied, thus the sacrifice and obligation ceased. Hebrews 10:16-18, "This is the covenant I will make with them after that time, says the Lord. I will put my laws in their hearts, and I will write them on their minds. Then he adds: Their sins and lawless acts I will remember no more." And where these have been forgiven, **there is no longer any sacrifice for sin**" (Holy Bible NIV).

Jesus fulfilled all of the prophecies of the Old Testament Prophets. During the remaining three-and-one half years, the disciples preached to the Jews first. Romans 1:16 makes it very clear that the Jews were first: "I am not ashamed of the gospel, because it is the power of God for the salvation of everyone who believes: **first for the Jew, then for the Gentile**" (Holy Bible NIV).

Jesus in Matthew 10:5-6 instructs the disciples: "Jesus sent these twelve out with the following orders. 'Do not go among those who aren't Jews,' he said. 'Do not enter any town of the Samaritans. Instead, go to the people of Israel. They are like sheep that have become lost.'" The disciples did exactly this until late 34 A.D. Three-and-one-half years after Jesus was crucified would be the end of going to the Jews first. Acts 8:5-8 records that Philip preached in Samaria: "Philip went down to a city in Samaria. There he preached about the Christ. The crowds listened to Philip. They saw the miraculous signs he did. They all paid close attention to what he said. Evil spirits screamed and came out of many people. Many who were disabled or who couldn't walk were healed. So there was great joy in that city." Did Philip disobey Christ? No, he knew the time when the seventy weeks were at an end. He went to Samaria to preach to the Gentiles with the full power of God. Acts 10 records Peter taking the Gospel to Caesarea. The Apostle Paul in Acts 13:46-49 clarifies that it was time for the Gospel to go to the Gentiles, "Then Paul and Barnabas answered them boldly: 'We had to speak the word of God to you first. Since you reject it and do not consider yourselves worthy of eternal life, we now turn to the Gentiles. For this is what the Lord has commanded us: I have made you a **light for the Gentiles**, that you may bring salvation to the ends of the earth.' When the Gentiles heard this, they were glad and honored the word of the Lord; and all who were appointed for eternal life believed. The word of the Lord spread through the whole region."

The disciples did abandon Jesus in the hour of His death on the cross as predicted by Daniel, centuries before the fact. The final piece of the prophecy states that the Romans, who are in power at the time of the last week, would be the ones destined and predicted to destroy the temple, the city of Jerusalem, and the rest of Israel. The disciples are aware of this and ask Jesus about it. **The Seventy Week prophecy did not give the date of the end of the Jews. Jesus provides the timeline of events that would befall the Jews.** The disciples asked Jesus two critical questions as they were leaving the temple.

70 WEEKS PROPHECY

7 WEEKS = 49 YEARS	62 WEEKS = 62 x 7 = 434 YEARS		
457 to 409 B.C. Jerusalem re-build during troubled times as predicted	409 B.C. to 26 A.D. The arrival of the Messiah is at the start of 70th Week	\multicolumn{2}{c}{70th WEEK}
		3 1/2 YRS 26-30 A.D. Christ Ministry to be 42 Months	3 1/2 YRS 30-34 A.D. Gospel to Jew First-42 Months
			144,000 are represented of Jews being saved first

TWO QUESTIONS

Matthew 24:1-3, "Jesus left the **temple** and was walking away when his disciples came up to him to call his attention to its buildings. 'Do you see all these things?' he asked. '**I tell you the truth, not one stone here will be left on another; every one will be thrown down.**' As Jesus was sitting on the Mount of Olives, the disciples came to him privately. 'Tell us,' they said, 'when will this happen, and what will be the sign of your coming and of the end of the age?'" The first and primary question that Jesus addressed was when the destruction of the temple would happen. He tells them that not one stone would be left on another. The second question was "What would be the sign of your coming and the end of the age?"

FIRST QUESTION
Before the Destruction of Temple
DECEIVERS ARE COMING

Matthew 24:4-5 "Jesus answered: 'Watch out that no one deceives you. For **many will come in my name**, claiming, I am the Christ, and will deceive many.'"

Before the destruction of the temple, deceivers would come. They came in mass just as Jesus predicted. Josephus, the noted Jewish historian, reports that a certain impostor named Thedeus, twelve years after the death of Christ, convinced a large following that he was the Christ and he would cause the river Jordan to divide for all those who followed him. In Acts 8, at the time of Felix, Judea was filled with impostors, whom Felix "put to death EVERYDAY" – a statement indicating that there were "many" of such in those days. Even an Egyptian gathered 30,000 followers to see him bring down the walls of Jerusalem. Then there is Simon, a sorcerer, who led people to believe he was a great power of God (Acts 8). According to Irenaeus, Simon claimed to be the Son of God. Origen mentions Dositheus, who claimed he was the Christ foretold by Moses. Jerome even shares that one called Barchochebas claimed to vomit flames. In Acts 13, Bar-Jesus, a sorcerer and false prophet, is mentioned. History confirms Jesus' words that there would be many deceivers.

WARS & RUMORS OF WAR ARE COMING

Matthew 24:6, "You will **hear of wars and rumors of wars**, but see to it that you are not alarmed. Such things must happen, but **the end is still to come.**"

When Jesus gave this prediction, the Roman Empire was experiencing a general peace and a period of relative stability within its borders. Did it change? Four Roman emperors came to sudden violent death in an eighteen-month period. Checking the Annals of Tacitus, a Roman who wrote a history of the period prior to 70 A.D., he describes exactly what Christ predicted. Listen to these descriptions: "Disturbances in Germany," Commotions in Africa," "Commotions in Thrace," Insurrections in Gaul," "Intrigues among Parthians," "War in Britain," and "War in Armenia." Locally, 50,000 Jews were killed in Seleucia. Another 20,000 died in Caesarea in battle with the Syrians. Then Caligula orders his statue to be placed in the Jewish Temple in Jerusalem. The Jews refuse and live in fear of punishment, so much so that many did not plant their crops. But, the end is not yet.

FAMINES AND EARTHQUAKES ARE COMING

Matthew 24:7-8, "Nation will rise against nation, and kingdom against kingdom. There will be **famines and earthquakes** in various places. All these are the beginning of birth pains."

The Bible records that there was famine "throughout all the world… in the days of Claudius Caesar" Acts 11:28. Historians Suetonius and Tacitus both record famines and pestilence throughout the empire. Eusebius mentions famines in Judea, Rome, and Greece. This is all prior to 70 A.D.

Seneca, writing in 58 A.D., said: "How often have the cities of Asia and Achaea fallen with one fatal shock! How many cities have been swallowed up in Syria! how many in Macedonia, how often has Cyrus been wasted by this calamity! How often has Paphos become ruin! News has often been brought us of the demolition of whole cities at once." In 63 A.D. Pompeii was hit. There were earthquakes in Crete, Apamea, Smyrna, Miletus, Samos, Judea, Laodocia, Colosse, Hierapous, and Campania. Even so, the end is not yet.

PERSECUTION & DEATH ARE COMING

Matthew 24:9-13: "Then you will be handed over to be **persecuted and put to death**, and you will be hated by all nations because of me. At that time **many will turn away from the faith** and will betray and hate each other, and many **false prophets will appear** and deceive many people. Because of the increase of wickedness, the love of most will grow cold, but he who stands firm to the end will be saved."

When Jesus told the Disciples that persecution and death were coming, they were still in the protection of Jesus and had no idea of what awaited them. Read Acts and it details exactly what Christ said would happen. They were brought before rulers – beaten, afflicted, killed, placed in prison, and martyred. History shows Jesus' words were fulfilled before the destruction of Jerusalem. When many who were weak in faith found out that Jesus' return was not imminent during their lifetime, there was a general falling away during the years leading up to 70 A.D.

GOSPEL PREACHED TO WHOLE WORLD

Matthew 24:14, "And this gospel of the kingdom will be **preached in the whole world** as a testimony to all nations, and then the end will come."

Act 2:5 states: "Godly Jews from every country in the world were staying in Jerusalem." They heard the gospel preached that day and 3,000 were converted. Thanks to Greek being the universal language and Rome's network of roads, the Gospel was able to go to the ends of the world. There would have not been a better time for the Disciples of Christ. As a Roman citizen, you were able to travel throughout the empire unimpeded. Once outside of its borders, being a Roman citizen afforded some degree of respect and protection. Even in the country of England, which would be considered the outermost reaches of the Roman Empire, the historian Newton said: "There is absolute certainty that Christianity was planted in this country in the days of the apostles, before the destruction of Jerusalem." In Rome, by the time of Nero in 64 A.D., the Christians had become so numerous that Nero tried to blame the fire of Rome on them. In Romans 1:8, the Apostle Paul mentions to Roman Christians that "Your faith is spoken of throughout the whole world." The message was that the Gospel had somehow entered every nation. This would happen prior to the destruction of the temple, just as Jesus predicted.

ABOMINATION OF DESOLATION TIME TO FLEE

Matthew 24:15-20, "So when you see standing in the holy place **'the abomination that causes desolation,**' spoken of through the prophet Daniel - let the reader understand - then let **those who are in Judea flee to the mountains.** Let no one on the roof of his house go down to take anything out of the house. Let no one in the field go back to get his cloak. How dreadful it will be in those days for pregnant women and nursing mothers! Pray that your flight will not take place in winter or on the Sabbath."

What is the Abomination of Desolation? There are three writers who recorded the same information from a unique perspective and with a different purpose. In the Gospel according to Luke, we find this event recorded in clear terminology. Luke 21:20-21, "A time is coming when you will see armies surround Jerusalem. Then you will know that it will soon be destroyed. Those who are in Judea should then escape to the mountains. Those in the city should get out. Those in the country should not enter the city." Daniel 9:26 told us it would be Roman armies and they would surround Jerusalem. The Abomination of Desolation is simply when Roman armies surround Jerusalem, then it is time to flee. <u>The Matthew Henry Commentary</u> states: "Jerusalem was the holy city, Canaan the holy land, the Mt. Moriah, which lay about Jerusalem, for its nearness to the temple was, they thought, in a particular manner holy ground; on the country lying round about Jerusalem the Roman army was encamped, that was the abomination that made desolate."[2] So the question is how does one flee if the city is surrounded? Expositors use history and prophecy to find the truth and to understand prophecy. Remember, the purpose of prophecy is that after the foretold event unfolds, we clearly see it. The pieces will all fit together without effort.

In 65 A.D., the Jews rebel and Cestius Gallus marches his armies to Jerusalem. After three days, he began the assault.[3] Seeing Jerusalem surrounded with Gentile armies, the disciples knew it was time to flee as Jesus told them. How? Cestius was an extremely successful commander and the Jews were ready to surrender. Suddenly, as Josephus recorded, "without any reason in the world" – Cestius withdrew his troops and departed! This filled the Jews with courage and they pursued the retreating army, inflicting on it a major disaster.[4] Adam Clarke wrote: "It is remarkable that not a single Christian perished in the destruction of Jerusalem though there were many there when Cestius Gallus invested [encompassed] the city." The Christians having seen the abomination of desolation (the Roman armies surrounded the holy city) departed Judea. This was an incredible fulfillment of prophecy.

THE GREAT TRIBULATION

Matthew 24:21-24, "For then there will be **great distress**, unequaled from the beginning of the world until now—and never to be equaled again. For then there will be **great tribulation** (affliction, distress, and oppression) such as has not been from the beginning of the world until now—no, and never will be [again]. If those days had not been **cut short, no one would survive**, but for the sake of the elect those days will be shortened. They will fall by the sword and will be taken as **prisoners to all the nations.** Jerusalem will be trampled on **by the Gentiles** until the times of the Gentiles are fulfilled."

Josephus, the Jewish historian who was witness to the destruction of Jerusalem, wrote a full and detailed account of the tribulation that fell upon the Jews in 70 A.D. His account, <u>War of the Jews</u>, was published in 75 A.D. The fact that Josephus was not a Christian removes the possibility of him slanting his account to match prophecy that Christ had given. Josephus said the calamities which befell the Jews were "the greatest of all those, not only that have been in our times, but in a manner, of those that ever were heard of; both of those wherein cities have fought against cities, or nations against nations… it appears to me that the misfortunes of all men, from the beginnings of the world, if they compared to these of the Jews, are not so considerable as they were."[5] The 20th Century scholar Boettner has well

---

[2]   Henry, Commentary on the Whole Bible, vol. 5, p. 352.
[3]   Josephus, Wars of the Jews, II, chapters 15-19.
[4]   Ibid, 19:5-8
[5]   Josephus, Preface, P. 427.

said: "There have been, of course, other periods of tribulation or suffering in which greater numbers of people were involved, and which continued for longer periods of time. But considering the physical, moral, and religious aspects, suffering never reached a greater **degree of awfulness and intensity** than in the siege of Jerusalem. Nor have so many people ever perished in the fall of any other city. We think of the **atomic bomb** that was dropped on Hiroshima as causing the greatest mass horror of anything in modern times. **Yet only about one-tenth** as many people were killed in Hiroshima as the fall of Jerusalem. Add to the slaughter of such a great number the bestiality of Jew to Jew and of Roman to Jew and the anguish of a people who knew they were forsaken of God, and we see the justification for Christ's words, "For then shall be great tribulation, such as hath not been seen from the beginning of the world until now, no, nor ever shall be."[6] In Jerusalem the Zealots, a Jewish faction, is recorded as bringing terror from within the walls. The Zealots "fell upon people as upon a flock of profane animals, cut their throats."[7] They slaughter 12,000 of the more eminent inhabitants. "Thus did the miseries of Jerusalem grow worse and worse every day… the multitude of carcasses that lay in heaps one upon another was a horrible sight, and produced a pestilential stench."[8] The prophecy of Deuteronomy 28:56-57 was fulfilled as predicted, "**The most gentle and sensitive woman among you**—so sensitive and gentle that she would not venture to touch the ground with the sole of her foot—will begrudge the husband she loves and her own son or daughter the afterbirth from her womb and the children she bears. For **she intends to eat them secretly during the siege** and in the distress that your enemy will inflict on you in your cities." One woman of prominence killed and roasted her infant son. When her house was entered by the seditious Jews in search of food, these hardened men were horrified at what she had done and left trembling. She showed them the remaining half of the body and said to them: "Come, eat do not pretend to be either more tender than a woman, or more compassionate than a mother."[9] This was recorded by non-Christians, showing the fulfillment of an extremely unique prophecy. Multiple events are required for us to know this. The prophecy must be given hundreds of years prior, the actual fulfillment must occur, followed by the recording of the events, and, finally, the preservation of this kind of evidence.

---

[6] Boettner, The Millennium, P. 202.
[7] Josephus, War of the Jews, IV, 5:3
[8] Josephus, War of the Jews, VI, 1:1
[9] Josephus, War of the Jews, VI, 3:4.

"Unless the days be shortened!" Finally, when the Roman army broke the wall they showed no mercy. There were a mere 97,000 left and over one million died in Jerusalem alone. Josephus recorded for us: "the populace was almost annihilated…there was no part of Judea, which did not partake of the calamities of the capital city."

Titus, the Roman Prince, wanted to spare the temple. However, the Jews are believed to have set the temple ablaze. The Romans fulfill Jesus' words that not one stone would be left on another. The Romans wanted the gold that had melted into the cracks of the temple's foundation. History records it took them 134 days to get the gold. After Gallus had retreated, Nero orders Vespasian to take over. Vespasian sends his son Titus, who brought the 5th and 10th Legions from Egypt and started the siege in 67 A.D.

ONE GENERATION

For prophecy to be true, Titus would need to become the Emperor's son, and Jerusalem's destruction must happen within one generation of Christ's death in 30 A.D. Matthew 24:32-35, "Now learn this lesson from the fig tree: As soon as its twigs get tender and its leaves come out, you know that summer is near. Even so, when you see all these things, you know that it is near, right at the door. I tell you the truth, **this generation will certainly not pass away until all these things have happened**. Heaven and earth will pass away, but my words will never pass away." A generation is forty years, which meant the Romans had to be victorious by 70 A.D. Why did the Romans not finish the job in 65 A.D.? Two reasons: first, the Christians needed to flee and be preserved. Second, the conqueror of Judea was to be a prince fulfilling Daniel's prophecies. Vespasian gets called to Rome for a crisis and becomes elevated to Emperor in 70 A.D. Titus now conquers Jerusalem and all of Judea as a prince. Here we again see the divine hand and timing of God.

FALSE PROPHETS ARE COMING

Matthew 24:23-28, "At that time if anyone says to you, 'Look, here is the Christ!' or, 'There he is!' do not believe it. For **false Christ's** and false prophets will appear and perform great signs and miracles to deceive even the elect—if that were possible. See, I have told you ahead of time. So if anyone tells you, 'There he is, out in the desert,' do not go out; or, 'Here he is, in the inner rooms,' do not believe it. For as **lightning that comes from the east is visible even in the west**, so will be the coming of the Son of Man. Wherever there is a carcass, there the vultures will gather."

In 1 John 4:1 we are warned that they are there: "Beloved, do not put faith in every spirit, but prove (test) the spirits to discover whether they proceed from God; for many **false prophets** have gone forth into the world" (Amplified Bible). By the time of his epistle to Titus, there were "many... deceivers." There are many verses describing false prophets as predicted. The key was to test them against the truth.

NIGHT FALLS ON THE JEWS

Matthew 24:29, "Immediately **after the distress of those days 'the sun will be darkened, and the moon will not give its light; the stars will fall from the sky, and the heavenly bodies will be shaken.'"**

The expressions of darkened, etc. are common figurative descriptions used by the prophets. The nation of Israel is promised bright days (blessings) if they were obedient to God; conversely, dark days (trouble, judgment) if disobedient. This type of symbolism is used throughout the Old Testament. We refer to the middle ages as the "Dark Ages." These symbols were used to portray divine truth and warnings and were within the framework of the established and sober language of those times. In this case, as history confirms, the light went out over Israel and their future became dark. No better description could be given of what was to be their lot for centuries.

DESTRUCTION OF JERUSALEM 70 A.D.
Overview of Gospels by Verse

Subject:	Matthew Chapter 24 Verses	Mark Chapter 13 Verses	Luke Chapter 21 Verses
Occasion of the address	1-3	1-4	5-7
Warnings against Deceivers	4-8	5-8	8-11
Persecution foretold	9-14	9-13	12-19
Destruction of Jerusalem	15-28	14-23	20-24
The coming of the Lord	30-31	24-27	25-28
Destruction of Temple	32-34	28-31	29-33

SECOND QUESTION ADDRESSED
CHRIST's RETURN

Matthew 24:30-31: "At that time the sign of the Son of Man will appear in the sky, and all the nations of the earth will mourn. They will see the Son of Man coming on the clouds of the sky, with power and great glory. And he will send his angels with **a loud trumpet call**, and they will gather his elect from the four winds, from one end of the heavens to the other."

God says He will show up and all nations will mourn. A loud trumpet announces His angels are coming to gather His elect.

THE DAY AND HOUR UNKNOWN

Matthew 24:36-44: "**No one knows about that day or hour**, not even the angels in heaven, nor the Son, but only the Father. As it was in the days of Noah, so it will be at the coming of the Son of Man. For in the days before the flood, people were eating and drinking, marrying and giving in marriage, up to the day Noah entered the ark; and they knew nothing about what would happen until the flood came and took them all away. That is how it will be at the coming of the Son of Man. Two men will be in the field; one will be taken and the other left. Two women will be grinding with a hand mill; one will be taken and the other left. "Therefore keep watch, because you do not know on what day your Lord will come. But understand this: If the owner of the house had known at what time of night the thief was coming, he would have kept watch and would not have let his house be broken into.

So you also must be ready, because the Son of Man will come at an hour when you do not expect him."

Jesus tells us something that has been disregarded century after century by Christians who want to play prophet. No one knows the day or hour of His return, not even Jesus. He clearly announces that only the Father knows. A word of caution regarding date setters: DISREGARD THEM!

We are going to look at recorded history. It will be for one main purpose: to focus upon Western Civilization's development and its impact on the God's Church. This history will be reviewed in comparison to Revelation in order to show God's complete control and sovereignty of all things. Man has free will. However, it is limited in that our free will fits into His will. A study of Western Civilization shows an epic battle over religious beliefs. Nations battled, and millions of people perished, over their choices and beliefs. History is recorded. Who, what, where, when, why, and how are the questions for which I sought answers.

Sir Isaac Newton 1642-1727, "The folly of interpreters has been to foretell times and things by this prophecy, as if God designed to make them prophets. By this rashness they have exposed themselves, but brought the prophecy also into contempt. The design of God was much otherwise. He gave this and the prophecies of the Old Testament not to foreknow things but that after they were fulfilled they might be interpreted by the event; and His wisdom be then manifested thereby to the world."

There is no desire to "play prophet" in this book, but rather to identify the fulfilled prophecy, thus showing God's divine control of all human affairs. Having lived through the last thirty years of the 20th Century, I have witnessed Christian authors/seers set dates and write books tied to daily events for the return of Christ and the end of the world. As we approached the year 2000 A.D., the expectation that we were living in the final days reached a feverish pitch. Were they tied to daily events to create sales or sensationalism?

History clearly shows a war between the Holy Roman Catholic Church and the non-Catholic believers covering many centuries. It is critical to understand that our history is our history. We cannot go back and change it. The purpose is to examine whether or not historical events match with Relevation in our search for truth. The Catholic church of the 21st Century is not the same as it was during the period when it was given both unlimited political and spiritual power for 1260 years in Europe. Today, the Catholic Church in America has the Scriptures read in English. Catholics today identify themselves as re-born Christians. Many of the Catholic priests are re-born. The Catholic Church today is considered part of the Christian community. This was not always true. There was a time when the Catholic Church was at war with true believers. The reformers of the 15th and 16th Century did not agree with the Catholic Church's doctrines. Martin Luther, who was trained to be a priest, rebelled against what he saw in the Catholic Church. Today, Catholics, along with their priests, have new freedoms to know the truth in Scripture. God identifies the old Holy Roman Catholic Church as the Beast. Today's Catholic Church is a weakened, unrepentant hierarchy. The Catholic Church has become exactly what God revealed. Revelation was provided for a reason. It shows the sovereignty of God and his control of all history. We start with a quick overview of various interpretations of Revelation.

SYSTEMS OF PROPHETIC INTERPRETATION

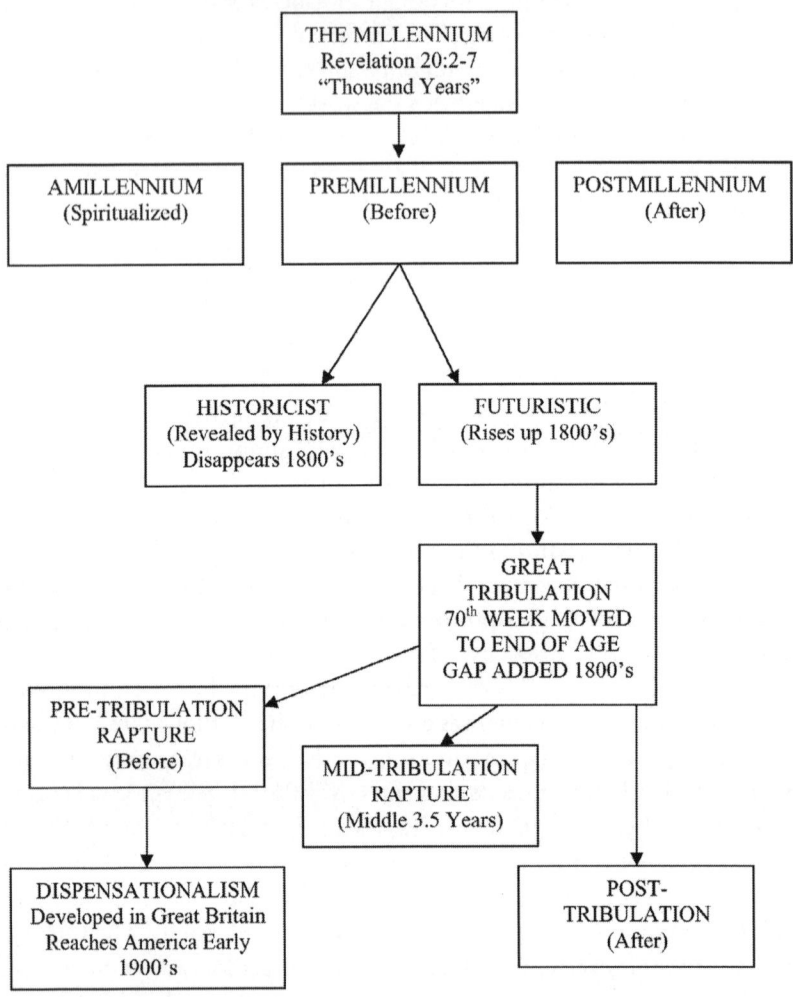

Christianity is essentially an historical religion. When it comes to history, the Bible is the perfect reference book since it has clearly shown that it has the Seal of God on it and is truly a revelation without error from God. The Bible would be used as the template, or roadmap, with which to compare history in order to see how God is working out His Plan.

We will do a quick review of the previous chart showing some of the major views of Revelation. It will surprise many in the church today that one of the greatest issues of controversy concerning the book of Revelation is the interpretation of the Millennium. The Apocalypse was defined in terms of one's understanding of the meaning of the "thousand years" referenced in Revelation Chapter 20.

The general assumption that the Millennium is to be taken literally as an actual 1,000 years is accepted by the masses as espoused by theologians. There are three major divisions: Premillennialism, Postmillennialism and Amillennialism. Premillennialism divides into historical and futurism views.

Amillennialism posits that the Millennium is an indefinitely long period of time. Proponents believe this period happens from the first advent of Christ to His second coming. Many great Christians from the early church right up to today have believed that the Millennium is not to be taken literally as 1,000 years, but was meant symbolically.

Postmillennium contends that Christ will return after the Millennium. The church is so successful that the world is converted and enters into an age of peace for a thousand years. Christ's second coming is at the end of this age of peace.

Premillennialism is the belief that the second coming of Christ is before the Millennium. This assumes that Christ, after His return, will set up His Kingdom on earth for 1,000 years. Satan is bound for that period of time, only to be released at the end of it. Man will be tested one more time.

Premillennialism separates into two major views. The Historic Premillennialism and Dispensationalism. Both views have been accused by their critics of promoting a pessimistic outlook of the future with the coming of Christ; however, for different reasons.

Historic Premillennialism believes that Revelation is a survey of church history. The early church knew that Rome would fall and that the Beast would rise on Rome. However, the development of historic views would begin in earnest during the reformation. The development of the historic view is seen in the works of Anselm of Havelberg (1129-1155), Rupert of Deutz (1111-1129), and even Joachim of Floris (1130-1201). Even though Joachim was loyal to the Church of Rome, he - and many who read his works - saw the Roman papacy as the Beast. These views were picked up by the Franciscans of the 13th and 14th Centuries, especially those in Paris. It was this link of the Beast to the Roman papacy that later galvanized the Reformers against the Papal system. Coming to the defense of the papacy was Francisco Ribera (1537-1591) and Luiz de Alcazar (1554-1613).

Luiz de Alcazar, a Jesuit scholar, introduced a Preterist approach to Revelation. It consisted of a three-part interpretation. In chapters 4-11, the Church battles Judaism, ending with the fall of Jerusalem in 70 A.D. Chapters 12-19 detail the church's struggle to overcome pagan Rome, which it wins in 326 A.D. Chapters 20-22 describe the rise and triumph of Papal Rome. We, being in the 21st Century, have the benefit of actual recorded history. It clearly shows this to be a false interpretation. Creative, but it was unable to remove Scripture's identification of the Papacy as the Beast. This version was never accepted by mainstream Christianity. A modified version of this preterist view is held by some today. The preterist view of the 21st Century believes Revelation was completely fulfilled upon the Jew during the destruction of Jerusalem. This totally ignores history and the fact that Revelation was written to the church and after 70 A.D.

Francisco Ribera, a professor at Salmanca, created an interpretation that declared John the Apostle only foresaw events of the near future and of the final things at the end of the world. Francisco Ribera defined the Antichrist as a future individual who would rise in the end times just before the return of Christ. Babylon was a future corrupted Rome, not the only true church presently headed by the popes.

Dispensationalism is probably today's most popular view, especially when you consider the phenomenally successful sales of books like Hal Lindsey's <u>The Late Great Planet Earth,</u> which easily exceeded twenty-five million copies. For almost two centuries, Protestants had regarded futurism as a product of the Roman Catholic Church and, in fact, it was. The first Protestant group to adopt any form of futurism was the Fifth Monarchy Men in the 17th Century. It was brought into disrepute and it was not until the 19th Century that the Plymouth Brethren recreated it with some new twists. John Darby, the leader of the Plymouth Brethren may not get the credit for the creation of Dispensationalism, but he was the key to what it became. Darby would change the 1,260 years found in Revelation to three-and-one-half years, which he joined to the 42 months found in a later chapter in Revelation, to produce a new seven-year period. Darby then linked this new seven-year period to the Great Tribulation. The Great Tribulation would now be a seven-year event according to Darby. This meant that Revelation no longer was to cover the church's history, but a final seven years. The next development Darby added was a secret rapture of the church prior to the Great Tribulation. It took Darby a few years to work out the details, but his final concept was to move the last week of Daniel's 70th week prophecy and make it part of the final seven years. The 70th week and the great tribulation become the same time period. The beast is an all-powerful super Antichrist. The 70th week was no longer about the Messiah, even though the prophecy clearly states its purpose as such. The Jews are now front and center as the focus of the end of time and not the church. Darby broke the 70th week prophecy into two pieces. The first sixty-nine weeks are in the past and are followed by a gap with the 70th week at the end of this age. This new concept rose partially as a result of the attacks of Theological Liberalism, as Higher Criticism spread.

I have presented Revelation as a sequence of events happening from 100 A.D. to the return of Christ. I do not fit into any of the known conventions above. Conspiracy theories do not interest me, only recorded historical events and how they compare to the revelation of God .

Most of the above interpretations start with the assumption that Revelation 20 must have a literal 1,000 year Millennium, except one. This has been for the most part the standard teaching for Introduction to Revelation 101 by the church for the past century. The question is why? The answer I found was that the majority have interpreted and believe it to be 1,000 literal years, so the thinking is that it must be true. Any interpretation based only on a single verse must be weighed against the whole of history and all of Scripture. You will read in this writing that on the last day of the world, at the return of Christ, the present earth and heavens are consumed by fire. This means that the standard interpretation may not be correct. That is why I applied the assumption that it would have to be compared to all of Scripture. The interpretation I chose was based on matching major events of the church's and the world's history to the whole of Scripture. My background and my education, along with the disquietude my spirit felt, provoked me to consider thinking outside the box. The hardest thing about seeking for truth is the elimination of previous knowledge, prejudices, and personal biases that everyone tends toward.

This interpretation shows that from chapter one to chapter eighteen is now history. Revelation 19-22 is in the future. It consists of the return of Christ, the end of this world, followed by the creation of the new heavens and earth.

100 A.D to 2000 A.D

The Old Testament and the New Testament have additional information that we will need to pull from in order to provide a complete picture. The book of Revelation will be used as the roadmap, and recorded history for verification of the fact that God has a plan for His Church, this world, and each of us.

We will begin with actually reading directly from Revelation. This approach provides a baseline from which to glean understanding. I am using the Holy Bible NIV translation unless otherwise indicated. There will be no verse breaks as they are disruptive to seeing the simple and clear reading as originally written.

REVELATION 1:1-3
Prologue

"The revelation of Jesus Christ, which God gave him to show his servants what must soon take place. He made it known by sending his angel to his servant John, who testifies to everything he saw—that is, the word of God and the testimony of Jesus Christ. Blessed is the one who reads the words of this prophecy, and blessed are those who hear it and take to heart what is written in it, because the time is near."

I usually like to state the obvious and keep the analysis at the macro level. My goal is to use the advantage of recorded history to determine the understanding of Revelation. This is the key to understanding at this juncture.

If God is in charge of all history and since history has happened within God's will, purpose, and plans, then events identified as important events in the book of Revelation that are in the past we should be able to identify and match to actual historical key turning points with the prophecy that was given by the Apostle John in Revelation. This is based on a simple assumption. The same God who wrote the book of Revelation also directed this world's history.

If you recall previously, asking the right question is critical. Start with the actual Scripture without the verse breaks, check the Old Testament and the New Testament for support and understanding, list what is clear, use history and non-biblical sources for additional clarification, and use commentaries and other help for context.

Review: Rev 1:1-3
Who is this book about? **Jesus Christ**
When must it take place? **Soon**
Who wrote it? **The Apostle John**
Those who read, hear, and take to heart are? **Blessed**

Revelation 1: 1-3 answers some simple but key questions. This book is about Jesus. Jesus is the central figure. What happens begins right away. The author was the Apostle John. Those who read it are blessed. Why are they blessed? By the end of this review of Revelation, I assume we will be able to uncover the truth God wants us to know about the future of this world.

DATING WRITING OF REVELATION

I wanted to find the best historical source for dating the writing of this book. The source that has the most credibility is the one closest to the writer (Apostle John) and his time of writing.

"Dionysius Barsalibi states that Hippolytus, like Irenaeus, holds the Apocalypse to have been written by John the Evangelist under Domitian" (Gwynn; Hermathena vii. P. 137). Irenaeus was born just thirty-five years after Domitian. Hippolytus, the student of Irenaeus, wrote in 200 A.D. and Irenaeus was intimate with Polycarp, who was the martyred disciple of the Apostle John. Eusebius is known as the Father of Church History. He quotes Irenaeus Book V. Irenaeus states:

"For it was not seen a long time back, but almost in my lifetime, at the end of Domitian's reign." We have that the Apostle John knew Polycarp, who knew Irenaeus, who knew Hippolytus and these are the men that Eusebius depended on for his histories. The overlap of their lives is important for us today. This establishes that REVELATION was written by the Apostle John after 79 A.D., Vespasian's death, but before 96 A.D., Domitian's death. There is no other non-biblical historical source document that carries more weight than this evidence. **The conclusion is that Revelation was written between 79 A.D. and 96 A.D.** The traditional date is 95 A.D., by the Apostle John on the Isle of Patmos (Rev 1:9).

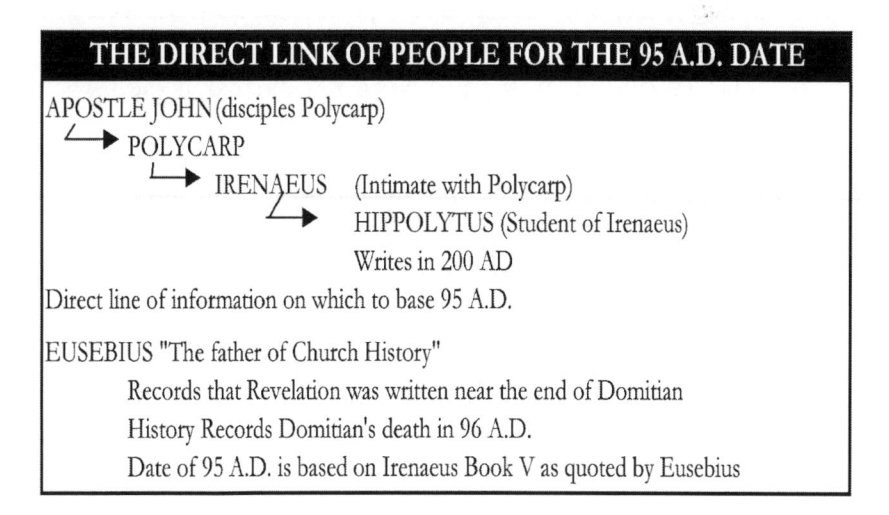

THE DIRECT LINK OF PEOPLE FOR THE 95 A.D. DATE

APOSTLE JOHN (disciples Polycarp)
↳ POLYCARP
   ↳ IRENAEUS   (Intimate with Polycarp)
      ↳ HIPPOLYTUS (Student of Irenaeus)
         Writes in 200 AD

Direct line of information on which to base 95 A.D.

EUSEBIUS "The father of Church History"
   Records that Revelation was written near the end of Domitian
   History Records Domitian's death in 96 A.D.
   Date of 95 A.D. is based on Irenaeus Book V as quoted by Eusebius

REVELATION 1:4-8
Greetings and Doxology

"John, To the **seven churches in the province of Asia**: Grace and peace to you from him who is, and who was, and who is to come, and from the seven spirits before his throne, and from Jesus Christ, who is the faithful witness, the firstborn from the dead, and the ruler of the kings of the earth. To him who loves us and has freed us from our sins by his blood, and has made us to be a kingdom and priests to serve his God and Father—to him be glory and power forever and ever! Amen. Look, **he is coming with the clouds**, and **every eye** will see him, even those who pierced him; and all the **peoples of the earth will mourn because of him**. So shall it be! Amen. 'I am the Alpha and the Omega,' says the Lord God, 'who is, and who was, and who is to come, the Almighty.'"

Review: Rev 1:4-8

To whom is the book written? It was to the **seven churches** in Asia. ***REVELATION IS WRITTEN TO, FOR, AND ABOUT THE FUTURE OF THE CHRISTIAN CHURCH.***
At His coming, **every eye will see Him** and all of the people **mourn**. Remember Matthew 24? It states the same reaction to His coming.

Review

Some believe (preterists) that Revelation was directed at the Jews and their destruction in 70 A.D. The reason for this is because Revelation does not mention the end of the Jews, so it is thought that it must have been written prior to Jerusalem's destruction.

First, this ignores the intent of the author. Revelation 1:4 states that Revelation was written to the church. Church tradition states that the Apostle John was banished during Domitian's 14th year. This would place the Apostle on the Isle of Patmos beginning 93 A.D. Nero did not exile or banish Christians like Domitian. Nero had them killed, many for sport.

Revelation would have been written between 79 A.D. and 96 A.D. This is important because it quickly helps to show that certain interpretations are not possible.

REVELATION 1:9-18

"I, John, your brother and companion in the suffering and kingdom and patient endurance that are ours in Jesus, was on the island of **Patmos** because of the word of God and the testimony of Jesus. On the Lord's Day I was **in the Spirit**, and I heard behind me a loud voice like a trumpet, which said: '**Write on a scroll what you see and send it to the seven churches**: to Ephesus, Smyrna, Pergamum, Thyatira, Sardis, Philadelphia and Laodicea.' I turned around to see the voice that was speaking to me. And when I turned I saw **seven golden lampstands**, and among the lampstands was someone **'like a son of man,'** dressed in a robe reaching down to his feet and with a golden sash around his chest. His head and hair were white like wool, as white as snow, and his eyes were like blazing fire. His feet were like bronze glowing in a furnace, and his voice was like the sound of rushing waters. In his right hand he held **seven stars**, and out of his mouth came a sharp double-edged sword. His face was like the sun shining in all its brilliance. When I saw him, I fell at his feet as though dead. Then he placed his right hand on me and said: 'Do not be afraid. I am the First and the Last. I am the Living One; I was dead, and behold I am alive forever and ever! And I hold the keys of death and Hades.'"

Review: Rev 1:9-18

Where is John? On the Island of **Patmos** located thirty-seven miles off Turkey's coast.
What is he doing? He is in the **Spirit**. What does "**In the Spirit**" mean in today's words? The Holy Spirit is providing John a vision of what He is to record under the direction and guidance of the Holy Spirit. It is how the other writers of the Holy Bible wrote.
Who are the **"Seven Stars"** and the **"Seven Golden Lampstands?"** Usually, Scripture will provide the answer and, in this case, it is following in Revelation 1:20. The seven stars are the **angels of God** and the Seven Golden Lampstands are the **seven churches**.
Who stood among the seven churches? someone "like the son of man." He stated, "I Am The First and The Last," which is another way of stating, "I am the Alpha and the Omega." Who is this person? **Jesus Christ**. Notice the way in which He is among His Churches. His church is comprised of believers and His Word states that, where two or three are gathered in His Name, He will be in their midst. This is consistent with what Jesus said.

REVELATION 1:19 OUTLINE FOR BOOK OF REVELATION

"Write, therefore, what you have seen, what is now and what will take place later. The mystery of the seven stars that you saw in my right hand and of the seven golden lampstands is this: The seven stars are the angels of the seven churches, and the seven lampstands are the seven churches."

Review: Rev 1:19 "THE OUTLINE"

John is to write –
1-What you have seen. This is the **recent past.**
2-What is now. This is the **present.**
3-What will take place later. This is the **future from the Apostle John's** perspective. It could be in the past from our perspective in the 21st Century.

From Revelation 1:1 "what must soon take place." This means that what John is writing will start being fulfilled. History supports this as evidenced by the following review of history and Revelation together.

RECENT PAST

The Apostle John wrote about what existed in his recent past. This covers the Seven Churches that would be a result of the other Apostles' Missionary efforts.

PRESENT

What is the Apostle John doing in "His" present? The apostle is being shown and told what to record. Revelation, Chapters Four and Five describe the present.

FUTURE

The Apostle John, from an historical timeline, records this prior to the death of Domitian. The future events began to unfold in a mere three years as described in Chapter Six of Revelation.

REVELATION 2: 1-7
To the Church in Ephesus

"To the angel of the church in Ephesus write: These are the words of him who holds the seven stars in his right hand and walks among the seven golden lampstands: I know your deeds, your hard work and your perseverance. I know that you cannot tolerate wicked men, that you have tested those who claim to be apostles but are not, and have found them false. You have persevered and have endured hardships for my name, and have not grown weary. Yet I hold this against you: You have forsaken your first love. Remember the height from which you have fallen! Repent and do the things you did at first. If you do not repent, I will come to you and remove your lampstand from its place. But you have this in your favor: You hate the practices of the Nicolaitans, which I also hate. He who has an ear, let him hear what the Spirit says to the churches. To him who overcomes, I will give the right to eat from the tree of life, which is in the paradise of God."

Review: Rev 2:1-7

Christ holds what against Ephesus?
You have forsaken your **first love**.

What does the **"OVERCOMER"** receive?
The ability to eat from the **Tree of Life**.

Most of us understand what is meant by first love. First love is that time of love in which we are overwhelmed with wanting to spend time with the one we love. Our thoughts and emotions are consumed. We do not tire of being together and when apart, we only look forward to being together again. God admonishes us to remember this first love we once had for Him. This is great advice for our personal lives as well.

REVELATION 2:8-11
To the Church in Smyrna

"To the angel of the church in Smyrna write: These are the words of him who is the First and the Last, who died and came to life again. I know your afflictions and your poverty - yet you are rich! I know the slander of those who say they are Jews and are not, but are a synagogue of Satan. Do not be afraid of what you are about to suffer. I tell you, the devil will put some of you in prison to test you, and you will suffer persecution for ten days. Be faithful, even to the point of death, and I will give you the crown of life. He who has an ear, let him hear what the Spirit says to the churches. He who overcomes will not be hurt at all by the second death."

Review: Rev 2:8-11

Christ knows their **afflictions and poverty, yet considers them rich!**

What is coming?
They will be tested, some will go to **prison,** and they will be **persecuted** for ten days. The number ten is the number of trial, testing, and responsibility. The round number here points to a short period which history shows did happen in the 1st Century. The Jews first persecuted the believers, followed by Nero in 64 A.D.

What does the **"OVERCOMER"** receive?
He will not suffer the second death. All men have to die the first death. However, those "in Christ" (in other words, re-born by faith having received Christ's atonement) will not die the second death. The first death is the physical that each of us face. The second death is at the end of this age after the return of Christ. All those who have never been re-born will be judged by their deeds before God. They will suffer the second death at this time. It is an eternity of banishment out of the presence of God forever. They appear before the GREAT WHITE THRONE. The Book of Life is opened to see if their names are in this Book. If their name is not in the Book of Life, their eternal fate has been determined by the decision they made about who Christ is and what they do with this knowledge prior to the first death (physical death). What you do now really does have eternal implications!

REVELATION 2:12-17
To the Church in Pergamum

"To the angel of the church in Pergamum write: These are the words of him who has the sharp, double-edged sword. I know where you live - where Satan has his throne. Yet you remain true to my name. You did not renounce your faith in me, even in the days of Antipas, my faithful witness, who was put to death in your city—where Satan lives. Nevertheless, I have a few things against you: You have people there who hold to the teaching of Balaam, who taught Balak to entice the Israelites to sin by eating food sacrificed to idols and by committing sexual immorality. Likewise you also have those who hold to the teaching of the Nicolaitans. Repent therefore! Otherwise, I will soon come to you and will fight against them with the sword of my mouth. He who has an ear, let him hear what the Spirit says to the churches. To him who overcomes, I will give some of the hidden manna. I will also give him a white stone with a new name written on it, known only to him who receives it." Christ was proud of them for what? they remained faithful under the threat of death.

Review: Rev 2:12-17

What are the things Christ has against them? Some are into Balaam worship with the eating of food sacrificed to idols and committing sexual immorality, which many times was a part of the ritual to their false gods. The teaching of the Nicolaitians did not make it to the 21st Century. All we know is that Christ warned them that He would come against them unless they repented from being involved.

What does the **"OVERCOMER"** receive? "I will give some of the **hidden manna**. I will also give him **a white stone with a new name written on it.**"

The manna indicates divine provision. The White Stone has two possible interpretations. One, it is referring back to the practice of the judge giving a white stone indicating acquittal or a black stone indicating condemnation. The other choice comes from the Greek games, where the contestants were given a white stone as they completed their race, which would be traded in for their actual reward. Either choice from historical context would be a plausible application.

REVELATION 2:18-29
To the Church in Thyatira

"To the angel of the church in Thyatira write: These are the words of the Son of God, whose eyes are like blazing fire and whose feet are like burnished bronze. I know your deeds, your love and faith, your service and perseverance, and that you are now doing more than you did at first. Nevertheless, I have this against you: You tolerate that woman Jezebel, who calls herself a prophetess. By her teaching she misleads my servants into sexual immorality and the eating of food sacrificed to idols. I have given her time to repent of her immorality, but she is unwilling. So I will cast her on a bed of suffering, and I will make those who commit adultery with her suffer intensely, unless they repent of her ways. I will strike her children dead. Then all the churches will know that I am he who searches hearts and minds, and I will repay each of you according to your deeds. Now I say to the rest of you in Thyatira, to you who do not hold to her teaching and have not learned Satan's so-called deep secrets (I will not impose any other burden on you): Only hold on to what you have until I come. To him who overcomes and does my will to the end, I will give authority over the nations - 'He will rule them with an iron scepter; he will dash them to pieces like pottery' - just as I have received authority from my Father. I will also give him the morning star. He who has an ear, let him hear what the Spirit says to the churches."

Review: Rev 2:18-29

Why is Thyatira rebuked? for allowing Jezebel, who calls herself a prophetess, "to lead my servants into **sexual immorality and the eating of food sacrificed to idols.**" Notice that most of the false religions developed from the "Mystery of Babylon Religion" coming down from Babel have idols (gods of stone, wood, etc), eating of food sacrificed to them, and sexual immorality, which was associated with serving their idols.

What does the **"OVERCOMER"** receive? Believers will be given authority over the nations. Exactly what kind and level of authority is not defined.

REVELATION 3:1-6
To the Church in Sardis

"To the angel of the church in Sardis write: These are the words of him who holds the seven spirits of God and the seven stars. I know your deeds; you have a reputation of being alive, but you are dead. Wake up! Strengthen what remains and is about to die, for I have not found your deeds complete in the sight of my God. Remember, therefore, what you have received and heard; obey it, and repent. But if you do not wake up, I will come like a thief, and you will not know at what time I will come to you. Yet you have a few people in Sardis who have not soiled their clothes. They will walk with me, dressed in white, for they are worthy. He who overcomes will, like them, be dressed in white. I will never blot out his name from the book of life, but will acknowledge his name before my Father and his angels. He who has an ear, let him hear what the Spirit says to the churches."

Review: Rev 3:1-6

What is wrong with this Church?
They are **dead** spiritually, dead in their love for God and Christ, not zealous. How many Sardis churches do we have in the 21st Century? The most important question is: do I belong to a dead church?

What does the **"OVERCOMER"** receive?
They will be **dressed in white;** translated, they receive the righteousness of God imputed to them as promised.

REVELATION 3:7-13
To the Church in Philadelphia

"To the angel of the church in Philadelphia write: These are the words of him who is holy and true, who holds the key of David. What he opens no one can shut, and what he shuts no one can open. I know your deeds. See, I have placed before you an open door that no one can shut. I know that you have little strength, yet you have kept my word and have not denied my Name. I will make those who are of the synagogue of Satan, who claim to be Jews though they are not, but are liars - I will make them come and fall down at your feet and acknowledge that I have loved you. Since you have kept my command to endure patiently, I will also keep you from the hour of trial that is going to come upon the whole world to test those who live on the earth. I am coming soon. Hold on to what you have, so that no one will take your crown. Him who overcomes I will make a pillar in the temple of my God. Never again will he leave it. I will write on him the name of my God and the name of the city of my God, the new Jerusalem, which is coming down out of heaven from my God; and I will also write on him my new name. He, who has an ear, let him hear what the Spirit says to the churches."

Review: Rev 3:7-13

What is the Church of Philadelphia rebuked for? **Nothing!**
The hour of trial against whom? This was the destruction of the Jews and the Great Tribulation event.

What does the **"OVERCOMER"** receive?
We are obviously not actually made into a pillar; we are to be with Christ in the New Jerusalem forever.

REVELATION 3:14-22
To the Church in Laodicea

"To the angel of the church in Laodicea write: These are the words of the Amen, the faithful and true witness, the ruler of God's creation. I know your deeds, that you are neither cold nor hot. I wish you were either one or the other! So, because you are lukewarm—neither hot nor cold—I am about to spit you out of my mouth. You say, 'I am rich; I have acquired wealth and do not need a thing.' But you do not realize that you are wretched, pitiful, poor, blind and naked. I counsel you to buy from me gold refined in the fire, so you can become rich; and white clothes to wear, so you can cover

your shameful nakedness; and salve to put on your eyes, so you can see. Those whom I love I rebuke and discipline. So be earnest, and repent. Here I am! I stand at the door and knock. If anyone hears my voice and opens the door, I will come in and eat with him, and he with me. To him who overcomes, I will give the right to sit with me on my throne, just as I overcame and sat down with my Father on his throne. He who has an ear, let him hear what the Spirit says to the churches."

Review: Rev 3:14-22

What is the Church of Laodicea rebuked for?
they are lukewarm; complacent in their wealth and lack of need.
What does the **"OVERCOMER"** receive?
We will rule with Him and He gives us the right to sit with him on His throne. If you recall, earlier in this book we discussed how God made us "joint heirs" with Christ and of all He has. This would include authority to rule with Him.

CHRIST STANDS AT THE DOOR

Christ restates His offer to **ALL**. In Revelation 3:20, "Here I am! I stand at the door and knock. **If anyone hears my voice and opens the door**, I will come in and eat with him, and he with me." The offer is to **ALL**. There are those in the church who believe and teach against this offer being for ALL. There is a doctrine that salvation is only for an elect group who has been pre-chosen by God and it matters not what we do. This is fatalism and removes man out of the equation, making history nothing more then a meaningless script. Yet, the prophets of God brought warnings and, depending on the people's responses, they received punishment and destruction or, if they repented, received His blessings. Decisions people make are in their control. How can God hold someone accountable for actions if they are not free? As people exercised their God-given free will, it somehow fit into the general and grand scheme of God's unfolding master plan for history. The how and why each person's individual decisions can work into God's overall plan is the privy of the Divine. The God of the Bible is an **INCLUSIVE GOD,** whosoever will. God is never EXCLUSIVE. Religion can be exclusive; man-made traditions can be exclusive; and, man-made doctrines can be exclusive. Scripture warns us to study the Word for ourselves. Why? Freedom from bondage; there are those who would like to keep us all under their control. John 8:32, **"The truth shall set you free!"** Are you free as God promised? Galatians 3:1-5, "You foolish Galatians! Who has bewitched you? Before your very eyes Jesus Christ was clearly portrayed as crucified. I would like to learn just one thing from you: Did you receive the Spirit **by observing the law, or by believing what you heard?** Are you so foolish? After beginning with the Spirit, are you **now trying to attain your goal by human effort?** Have you suffered so much for nothing - if it really was for nothing? Does God give you his Spirit and work miracles among you because you observe the law, or because you believe what you heard?" The Galatians started off by faith in Christ, then the Christian Jews were adding the keeping of the Law back on top of the grace and freedom of God. Jesus said His yoke was light! Today, for the majority of our religions, the yoke is not light. One can be saved, yet be carrying a heavy yoke for no reason. Religious organizations add requirements to what God clearly expects from us. If you carry a heavy burden or yoke turn to Scripture and God for freedom. This is the end of the past from the Apostle's viewpoint.

REVELATION 4
The Throne in Heaven

"After this I looked, and there before me was a door standing open in heaven. And the voice I had first heard speaking to me like a trumpet said, 'Come up here, and I will show you what must take place after this.' **At once I was in the Spirit, and there before me was a throne in heaven** with someone sitting on it. And the one who sat there had the appearance of jasper and carnelian. A rainbow, resembling an emerald, encircled the throne. Surrounding the throne were twenty-four other thrones, and seated on them were twenty-four elders. They were dressed in white and had crowns of gold on their heads. From the throne came flashes of lightning, rumblings and peals of thunder. Before the throne, seven lamps were blazing. These are the seven spirits of God. Also before the throne there was what looked like a sea of glass, clear as crystal. In the center, around the throne, were four living creatures, and they were covered with eyes, in front and in back. The first living creature was like a lion, the second was like an ox, the third had a face like a man, the fourth was like a flying eagle. Each of the four living creatures had six wings and was covered with eyes all around, even under his wings. Day and night they never stop saying: 'Holy, holy, holy is the Lord God Almighty, who was, and is, and is to come.' Whenever the living creatures give glory, honor and thanks to him who sits on the throne and who lives for ever and ever, the twenty-four elders fall down before him who sits on the throne, and worship him who lives for ever and ever. They lay their crowns before the throne and say: 'You are worthy, our Lord and God, to receive glory and honor and power, for you created all things, and by your will they were created and have their being.'"

> **This is a vision to be read and enjoyed.**
>
> Imagine if we could see it. What would it be like?
> Who can explain this revelation with any certainty?
> There are books listed in the suggested reading section that are full of analysis and opinions.

REVELATION 5
The Enthronement Of Christ

"When I saw in the right hand of him who sat on the throne a scroll with writing on both sides and sealed with seven seals. And I saw a mighty angel proclaiming in a loud voice, 'Who is worthy to break the seals and open the scroll?' But no one in heaven or on earth or under the earth could open the scroll or even look inside it. I wept and wept because no one was found who was worthy to open the scroll or look inside. Then one of the elders said to me, 'Do not weep! See, the **Lion of the tribe of Judah, the Root of David, has triumphed.** He is able to open the scroll and its seven seals.' Then I saw a **Lamb, looking as if it had been slain**, standing in the center of the throne, encircled by the four living creatures and the elders. He had seven horns and seven eyes, which are the seven spirits of God sent out into all the earth. He came and took the scroll from the right hand of him who sat on the throne. And when he had taken it, the four living creatures and the twenty-four elders fell down before the Lamb. Each one had a harp and they were holding golden bowls full of incense, which are the prayers of the saints. And they sang a new song: 'You are worthy to take the scroll and to open its seals, because you were slain, and with **your blood you purchased men for God from every tribe and language and people and nation.** You have made them to be a kingdom and priests to serve our God, and they will reign on the earth.' Then I looked and heard the voice of many angels, numbering thousands upon thousands, and ten thousand times ten thousand. They encircled the throne and the living creatures and the elders. In a loud voice they sang: **'Worthy is the Lamb, who was slain, to receive power and wealth and wisdom and strength and honor and glory and praise!'** Then I heard every creature in heaven and on earth and under the earth and on the sea, and all that is in them, singing: **'To him who sits on the throne and to the Lamb be praise and honor and glory and power, for ever and ever!'** The four living creatures said, 'Amen,' and the elders fell down and worshiped.'"

> This shows us the **enthronement of the Lamb, Jesus Christ.** He is from the tribe of Judah, the Root of David, and He has won the war. His blood has purchased people from every tribe, language, and nation. He has made us part of the Kingdom of God and we have become His priests. He is the One who can open the "Scroll." Again this is to be read and enjoyed by us. This second part is the Apostle John's present.

REVELATION 6 The Seals
1st SEAL - HERE COMES THE WHITE HORSE

Revelation 6:1-2 "I watched as the Lamb opened the first of the seven seals. Then I heard one of the four living creatures say in a voice like thunder, 'Come!' I looked, and there before me was a white horse! Its rider held a bow, and he was given a crown, and he rode out as a conqueror bent on conquest."

> ### CLUES: Rev 6:1-2
>
> Who opened the seven seals? **The Lamb (Jesus Christ)**
>
> The **first seal** is represented by a **White Horse.**

Remember the outline from Revelation 1:19. The Apostle John covers events in his past in chapters 1-3. He covers events that are happening to him at the present moment of writing in chapters 4-5. This chapter begins the Apostle John's unveiling of the Church's future. It is important to note that we need to be thinking as if we are in the 1st Century. We are under the authority of Rome. The Apostle Paul had clearly warned the body of Christ in veiled terms that Rome would have to pass away for a man of lawlessness was coming. II Thessalonians 2:6-7, "And now you know what is holding him back, so that he may be revealed at the proper time. For the secret power of lawlessness is already at work; but the one who now holds it back will continue to do so until he is taken out of the way." Let's see what some of the early Christians understood.

Irenaeus writes on the future and he begins with: "John and Daniel have predicted the dissolution of the Roman Empire, which shall precede the end of the world..." They did not know who would rise up from Rome's ashes.

> **The best way is to wait and see. History fulfills prophecy and one only needs to be watchful!**

Jerome, one of the early church's greatest spiritual fathers, writes on II Thessalonians, Chapter Two. He has the advantage of the passage of time. When John wrote Rome was at peace, Jerome saw the beginning of Rome's woes and wrote "...unless the Roman Empire be first desolated, and the antichrist precede, Christ shall not come." Jerome had a clear understanding from Daniel, II Thessalonians, and Revelation that certain things had to occur.

> The early Christian fathers understood Christ would not return until Rome fell and the man of lawlessness, the antichrist spirit would rise up.

White is the symbol of something good, the bow and crown of armored authority, and expansion of territory in conquest. This prophecy states that the next period in Rome, after the reign of Domitian, will be one that is good for Rome, with expansion through conquest.

HISTORICAL FULFILLMENT:

Looking to secular history; do we find what Scripture has revealed? This period of time is known as the **Pax Romana,** or translated Peace of Rome. It is also known as the period of the five Good Emperors (98 – 180 A.D.). It is characterized by conquest as predicted in revelation. In fact, Rome's expansion was to its greatest limits. Revelation said it would be a good time for Rome and a time of conquest. This was what history has recorded.

The four horsemen indicate that they should be concerning the same entity. This gives the expectation that the next three horses would apply to Rome as well.

2nd SEAL - HERE COMES THE RED HORSE

Revelation 6:3-4, "When the Lamb opened the second seal, I heard the second living creature say, 'Come!' Then another horse came out, a fiery red one. Its rider was given power to take peace from the earth and to make men slay each other. To him was given a large sword."

CLUES: Rev 6:3-4

Who opened the seal? **the Lamb**
What came? **a fiery red horse**
What power does it have? **takes peace from the earth**
What was he given? **the sword**

The **second seal** is represented by a **Red Horse.**

The Final Trumpet

Red is the symbol of blood, war, and fire. Peace would disappear and they would slay each other with the "Sword." This reveals that Rome's next period is the opposite of the first period. They will not have peace in the Empire and they **will slay each other**, indicating **internal strife and civil war** will come upon Rome.

HISTORICAL FULFILLMENT:

Looking to secular history; do we find what Scripture has revealed? Rome's next period was known as the period of Disorder (180-270 A.D.). Imagine eighty Emperors in a period of just ninety years with most of them dying violently. The empire fell into a series of civil wars, leading to whomever had an army would march on Rome and take the post as Emperor until defeated by the next army. This brought disruption and destruction to the Empire causing even basic items to halt, like the planting of crops, depletion of stockpiles, and a general breakdown of society, as well as burning of the countryside, Did they slay each other with the sword? Yes, repeatedly. Rome fell into civil war just as Scripture foretold.

3rd SEAL - HERE COMES THE BLACK HORSE

Revelation 6:5-6, "When the Lamb opened the third seal, I heard the third living creature say, 'Come!' I looked, and there before me was a black horse! Its rider was holding a pair of scales in his hand. Then I heard what sounded like a voice among the four living creatures, saying, 'A quart of wheat for a day's wages, and three quarts of barley for a day's wages, and do not damage the oil and the wine!'"

CLUES: Rev 6:5-6

Who opened the seal? **the Lamb**
What came? **a black horse**
What power does it have? **a pair of scales**
What is indicated? **a day's wages for some food**

The third seal is represented by a Black Horse.
Black is the symbol of darkness and despair. The high prices for items point out shortages, indicating a period of famine and hard times.

HISTORICAL FULFILLMENT:

Looking to secular history, do we find what Scripture has revealed? The third period was famine and shortages to the empire as predicted. Things were bad. "Lacking money the government paid soldiers in land, and **received taxes in grain**...the army through force put incompetent rulers in power... Wasteful methods of villa farming led to decreased productiveness." This is just the opposite from earlier periods. When an earthquake destroyed a city, Rome would come with aid and quickly rebuild and sustain them until they were self-sufficient again. **The Empire had entered a period of hard times as predicted.** Behind famines typically follow pestilence and death. This period began in the late 3rd Century. Where this prophecy ends is difficult to pinpoint because the next rider (Death) is the result of this rider. There would naturally be overlap because famine brings death.

4th SEAL - HERE COMES THE PALE HORSE

Revelation 6:7-8 "When the Lamb opened the fourth seal, I heard the voice of the fourth living creature say, "Come!" I looked, and there before me was a pale horse! Its rider was named Death, and Hades was following close behind him. They were given power over a fourth of the earth to kill by sword, famine and plague, and by the wild beasts of the earth.

CLUES: Rev 6:7-8

Who opened the seal? **the Lamb**
What came? **a pale horse**
What is his name? **death!**

The fourth seal is represented by a Pale Horse.
Pale is the symbol of sickliness. This symbol points to death. A fourth part of the earth is to die from the sword, famine, disease, and wild animals. The Roman Empire is to have a major depopulation.

The Final Trumpet

> ## HISTORICAL FULFILLMENT:
>
> Looking to secular history, do we find what Scripture has revealed? Gibbon writes from the years 248 to 296 A.D., "five thousand persons died daily in Rome; and many towns that escaped the hands of the barbarians were entirely depopulated." Eusebius records for us information about wild animals. "Death waged a desolating war with …famine and pestilence… Man wasted away to mere skeletons, stumbling hither and thither like mere shadows, trembling and tottering. They fell down in the midst of the streets… Some indeed already the food for dogs." Rome was to reap the consequences of the preceding civil wars and it was a dear price. Due to the depopulation and utter devastation inflicted on the Empire, even wild animals turned deadly in once civilized areas, and the deaths from animal attacks were common enough to be reported in the Roman histories. There was an outbreak of the black plague (bubonic plague) at this time. It is a certainty that the Empire lost a minimum of one-quarter of its population. Some estimates believe it was as high as one-half. The fulfilled prophecy and the dating of this period's end is best determined by the start of the next prophecy and period of history. Based on known historical information, this period of depopulation would have ended near or just before 300 A.D.

5th SEAL–SAINTS PERSECUTED & SLAIN ENDS

Revelation 6:9-11: "When he opened the fifth seal, I saw under the altar the souls of those who had been slain because of the word of God and the testimony they had maintained. They called out in a loud voice, 'How long, Sovereign Lord, holy and true, until you judge the inhabitants of the earth and avenge our blood?' Then each of them was given a white robe, and they were told to wait a little longer, until the number of their fellow servants and brothers who were to be killed as they had been was completed."

> ## CLUE: Rev 6:9-11
>
> What did he see? The souls of those **who had been slain.**

> ## HISTORICAL FULFILLMENT:
>
> Who do you think Rome blamed for the troubles of the Empire? The Christians, and Rome felt they needed to be dealt with harshly. The **saints of God being persecuted and killed represent the fifth seal**, but it will come to an end and it is the last one. Based on the prophecy, it indicates an expectation of an intense and short time of persecution. Looking to secular history, do we find what Scripture has revealed? History records the tenth and worst persecution of Christians by the Empire. "In February, 303, the four rulers decreed the destruction of all churches, the burning of Christian books, the dissolution of Christian congregations, the confiscation of their property, the exclusion of Christians from public office, and the punishment of death for Christians detected in religious assembly. A band of soldiers inaugurated the persecution by burning to ground the cathedral at Nicomedia." This last and most severe persecution caused the deaths of thousands of saints, the burning of churches, and the burning of Bibles. Every elder/bishop who was found was arrested and killed. It was back in fashion to use Christians as sport in arenas. Diocletian resigned in 304 A.D. to leave his son-in-law, Galerius, in charge, who then issued the Edict of Persecution. This period was called by Tertullian "The Blood of Martyrs." Diocletian weakened the church temporarily. After eight years of brutalities, the result was that the pagan population and Roman citizens were stirred up against the emperor's edict to the point where they began hiding the Christians. Again, we see that history and Revelation seem to be in line with one another.

6th SEAL – THE WORLD TURNS UPSIDE DOWN

Revelation 6:12-17; "I watched as he opened the sixth seal. There was a great earthquake. The sun turned black like sackcloth made of goat hair, the whole moon turned blood red, and the stars in the sky fell to earth, as late figs drop from a fig tree when shaken by a strong wind. The sky receded like a scroll, rolling up, and every mountain and island was removed from its place. Then the kings of the earth, the princes, the generals, the rich, the mighty, and every slave and every free man hid in caves and among the rocks of the mountains. They called to the mountains and the rocks, 'Fall on us and hide

The Final Trumpet

us from the face of him who sits on the throne and from the wrath of the Lamb! For the great day of their wrath has come, and who can stand?'"

The sixth seal is represented by a great earthquake with the sun, moon, stars, mountains, and islands being impacted and changed. It affected kings, princes, generals, rich, mighty, slave, and every free man. The one who brings the change sits on the throne and is the Lamb, an obvious reference to Christ, "The Lamb of God." For the day of wrath has come on those in religious power. The pagans' religions in this next period appear to be impacted. The sun and moon represent authority. The stars falling from the sky indicate the apostate beliefs are going to fall. The moon going dark indicates from Scripture that light will shine through darkness; in this case probably the Church overcomes. Mountains always represented a symbol of strength, majesty, and stability, whether talking about kingdoms, man, or God. Since the verses state they are "removed from its place," would suggest that stability is turned upside down by the Lamb.

HISTORICAL FULFILLMENT:

Looking to secular history; do we find what Scripture has revealed? "There is no greater drama in human record than the sight of a few Christians, scorned or oppressed by a succession of emperors, bearing all trials with a fierce tenacity, multiplying quietly, building order while their enemies generated chaos, fighting the sword with the word, brutality with hope, and at last defeating the strongest state that history has ever known. **Caesar and Christ had met in the arena, and Christ had won**" How could this happen? How could the pagan religions fall and Christianity be elevated to the **OFFICIAL RELIGION** of the Empire. Galerius, on succeeding Diocletaian, moved to assert his heredity claims to the throne.
1 Durant, Will, The Story Of Civilization, Caser and Christ, Vol. 3, P. 652.

FULFILLMENT (cont.):

Constantine, who was a young officer in Rome, escaped from his watchers and rode night and day until joining his father Constantius in the British campaign. The Gallic army, deeply loyal to the humane Constantius, felt the same about Constantine. So, when his father died at York, they recognized him as Caesar and Augustus – Emperor in 306 A.D. Galerius, too distant to affect this turn of events, reluctantly recognized him as a Caesar. Constantine and his father never followed the rest of the empire in the persecution of the Christians. Resultant, his armies had many Christians and he saw their immediate and long-term value to the empire by bringing their high level of ethics, which was something Rome had lost. By 307, there were six Caesars and one Emperor, Calerius; who died in 311. Constantine's conversion was either an act of religious belief or a stroke of political genius. Helena, his mother, became a Christian and is said to have acquainted her son with the truth of the invisible God.

On October 27, 312, Constantine met the forces of Maxentius at Saxa Rubra (Red Rocks) nine miles north of Rome. On the afternoon prior to the battle, Constantine saw a flaming cross in the sky, with the Greek words "en toutoi nika" – "in this sign conquer." His soldiers were supposedly told to put a cross upon their shields. Maxentius makes a critical error in strategy and was caught with his back against the Tiber with no retreat possible except over the Mulvian Bridge. Constantine forces secured the bridge and Maxentius perished in the Tiber along with thousands of his troops. Early in 313, Constantine and Licinius met in Milan to work out their rule. Constantine and Licinius issued the "Edict of Milan." This ordered the return of Christians' property and rights and the incredible elevation of **Christianity as the empire's official religion.** The world had been turned upside down and, for the first time in history, the pagan religions were no longer in charge. A simple reading of the actual Scriptures, with the standard symbolic meaning applied and compared to history using common sense shows truth where history and prophecy agreed since both are controlled by the God of this universe. Should we be surprised? The period from Constantine to 460 A.D is known in secular history as the **rise of the Christian church.**

REVELATION 7:1-8
SEALING THE 144,000

"After this I saw four angels standing at the four corners of the earth, holding back the four winds of the earth to prevent any wind from blowing on the land or on the sea or on any tree. Then I saw another angel coming up from the east, having the seal of the living God. He called out in a loud voice to the four angels who had been given power to harm the land and the sea: 'Do not harm the land or the sea or the trees until we put a seal on the foreheads of the servants of our God.' Then I heard the number of those who were sealed: 144,000 from all the tribes of Israel. From the tribe of Judah 12,000 were sealed, from the tribe of Reuben 12,000, from the tribe of Gad 12,000, from the tribe of Asher 12,000, from the tribe of Naphtali 12,000, from the tribe of Manasseh 12,000, from the tribe of Simeon 12,000, from the tribe of Levi 12,000, from the tribe of Issachar 12,000, from the tribe of Zebulun 12,000, from the tribe of Joseph 12,000, from the tribe of Benjamin 12,000."

CLUE: Rev 7:1-8

Four angels were holding back what? **They were holding back the four winds from blowing on the land or sea**
What will be affected? **The land and sea**
Do no harm until? **The 144,000 are sealed**
Who are the 144,000? **12,000 from each Tribe**

Who is this section about? The **servants of God** are sealed on their foreheads.

Who are they? They are from the **tribes of Israel.**

How many? **144,000**

Where are they from? There are **12,000** symbolic representatives from each of the **twelve tribes** of Israel.

Chapter fourteen has one critical element that is the key to understanding the identification of the 144,000 found here in chapter seven.

Revelation 14:1-5 "Then I looked, and there before me was the Lamb, standing on Mount Zion, and with him 144,000 who had his name and his Father's name written on their foreheads. And I heard a sound from heaven like the roar of rushing waters and like a loud peal of thunder. The sound I heard was like that of harpists playing their harps. And they sang a new song before the throne and before the four living creatures and the elders. No one could learn the song except the 144,000 who had been redeemed from the earth. These are those who did not defile themselves with women, for they kept themselves pure. They follow the Lamb wherever he goes. They were purchased from among men and offered as firstfruits to God and the Lamb. No lie was found in their mouths; they are blameless."

FIRSTFRUITS!

Did you see the key that was not given in chapter seven? **FIRSTFRUITS!**

Let's go to the Bible to see what is meant by firstfruits and compare this to the whole of Scripture. In the Old Testament, the term "firstfruits" meant the FIRST gathering of the crops, which were presented to the Lord (Ex. 23:19, Lev. 2:14 and Neh. 10:35). In the New Testament, Jesus Christ, who was "the first that should rise from the dead" to immortality (Act 26:23), is called **"the FIRSTFRUITS of them that slept"** (1 Cor. 15:20). The first converts in Achaia were called **"the firstfruits"** (1 Cor. 16:15). So, who are the 144,000? the symbolic representation of the first Jews saved. Do you remember Roman 1:16? **The gospel went to the Jews first and then to the Gentiles.** (This was part of the seventy-week prophecy; that the second half of the seventieth week the Gospel would go the Jews for three and one half years first.) The next chapter is about the Great Multitude from ALL NATIONS, including Jews. This covers all saints from the beginning of the Church until the end of this present age. The event that ends this age is the return of Christ at the last trumpet.

REVELATION 7:9-17
The Great Multitude in White Robes

"After this I looked and there before me was a great multitude that no one could count, from every nation, tribe, people and language, standing before the throne and in front of the Lamb. They were wearing white robes and were holding palm branches in their hands. And they cried out in a loud voice: 'Salvation belongs to our God, who sits on the throne, and to the Lamb.' All the angels were standing around the throne and around the elders and the four living creatures. They fell down on their faces before the throne and worshiped God, saying: 'Amen! Praise and glory and wisdom and thanks

The Final Trumpet

and honor and power and strength be to our God forever and ever. Amen!' Then one of the elders asked me, 'These in white robes - who are they, and where did they come from?' I answered, 'Sir, you know.' And he said, 'These are they who have come out of the great tribulation; they have washed their robes and made them white in the blood of the Lamb.'

Therefore, they are before the throne of God and serve him day and night in his temple; and he who sits on the throne will spread his tent over them. Never again will they hunger; never again will they thirst. The sun will not beat upon them, nor any scorching heat. For the Lamb at the center of the throne will be their shepherd; he will lead them to springs of living water. And God will wipe away every tear from their eyes."

CLUE: Rev 7:9-17

What did the apostle see standing before the throne?
A great multitude that no one could count from every nation
What did they have on? **White Robes**
Where were they from? **The great tribulation**

Who is this section about? **A great multitude in White Robes**
Who are they? **Believers in heaven who are before the throne**
Why white robes? **They represent the righteousness of Jesus** applied to the believer. It is how God sees us. We are the redeemed in Christ. God sees us as sinless because of Christ.
Where are they from? **The great tribulation**
When was this great tribulation? **It started on the day of Pentecost and will end at the second coming of Christ.** The key is that this section states every nation, people, and language will be present – everyone is there. As believers, why would God have this section? It shows that God is going to have a multitude of saints that no one can count. It shows that the Lamb has conquered all. It provides hope, strength, and motivation to any believer who reads it. It does exactly what the prologue to Revelation said it would do for us. **It blesses us.** Jesus Christ will be our shepherd and we will drink of living water. God will wipe away every tear from our eyes. This is to be read and enjoyed by us, the purchased of God.

REVELATION 8:1-5
The Seventh Seal and the Golden Censer

"When he opened the seventh seal, there was silence in heaven for about half an hour. And I saw the seven angels who stand before God, and to them were given seven trumpets. Another angel, who had a golden censer, came and stood at the altar. He was given much incense to offer, with the prayers of all the saints, on the golden altar before the throne. The smoke of the incense, together with the prayers of the saints, went up before God from the angel's hand. Then the angel took the censer, filled it with fire from the altar, and hurled it on the earth; and there came peals of thunder, rumblings, flashes of lightning and an earthquake."

CLUES: Rev 8:1-5

What is opened? **The seventh seal**
What appears after the seventh seal is opened? **Seven angels with seven trumpets**
What did the other angel have? **A censer that he hurled to earth**

The seventh seal is opened. It contained seven angels with seven trumpets. We will see that the first four seals all pertain to Rome and the question becomes: Is God finished with the Roman Empire? II Thessalonians, Chapter Two, clearly warned the early Christians that the "**Man of Lawlessness**" must come and that the only thing holding him back was the Roman Empire. After Rome fell, he would appear. The Apostle Paul obviously used veiled language here, but the early church knew the intent of the message.

2 THESSALONIANS 2:1-12
The Man of Lawlessness

"Concerning the coming of our Lord Jesus Christ and our being gathered to him, we ask you, brothers, not to become easily unsettled or alarmed by some prophecy, report or letter supposed to have come from us, saying that the day of the Lord has already come. Don't let anyone deceive you in any way, for that day will not come until the rebellion occurs and the man of lawlessness is revealed, the man doomed to destruction. He will oppose and will exalt himself over everything that is called God or is worshiped, so that he sets himself up in God's temple, proclaiming himself to be God. Don't you remember that when I was with you I used to tell you these things? And now you know what is holding him back, so that he may be revealed at the proper time. For the secret power of lawlessness is already at work; but the one who now holds it back will continue to do so until he is taken out of the way. And then the lawless one will be revealed, whom the Lord Jesus will overthrow with the breath of his mouth and destroy by the splendor of his coming. The coming of the lawless one will be in accordance with the work of Satan displayed in all kinds of counterfeit miracles, signs and wonders, and in every sort of evil that deceives those who are perishing. They perish because they refused to love the truth and so be saved. For this reason God sends them a powerful delusion so that they will believe the lie and so that all will be condemned who have not believed the truth but have delighted in wickedness."

CLUES: II Thessalonians 1:1-12

Who is coming? **The Man of Lawlessness**
Whom does he opose? **God**
Why has he delayed? **He is being restrained**

He would come except "...the **one** who now holds it back will continue to do so until he is taken out of the way." **One** here indicates the Roman Empire. What will the Man of Lawlessness do? He will substitute himself in place of God. He will **call himself God** and be considered divine. He will do counterfeit miracles, signs, and wonders. The people perish because? **they believe a lie.**

Listen to St. John Chrysostom in the late Fourth Century as he writes on II Thessalonians 2:6-9. Here is what he reveals: "What is that which withholds?" and "why does Paul expresses it so obscurely. What then hinders him from being revealed? Some indeed say the grace of the Spirit, but others the **Roman Empire**, to whom I most of all accede. Because if he meant the Spirit, he would not have spoken obscurely, but plainly, that, even now the grace of the Spirit, that is, the gifts, withhold him. Otherwise he ought now to have come, if he was about to come when the gifts ceased; for they have long since ceased!"[10]

Where is this Man of Lawlessness going to sit? Daniel 7 has that answer. Daniel 7:23-27, "He gave me this explanation: 'The fourth beast is a **fourth kingdom** that will appear on earth. It will be different from all the other kingdoms and will devour the whole earth, trampling it down and crushing it. The ten horns are **ten kings who will come from this kingdom**. After them another king will arise, different from the earlier ones; he will subdue three kings. He will **speak against** the Most High and **oppress his saints** and try to **change the set times and the laws**. The saints will be handed over to him **for a time, times and half a time**. But the court will sit, and his power will be taken away and completely destroyed forever. Then the sovereignty, power and greatness of the kingdoms under the whole heaven will be handed over to the saints, the people of the Most High. His kingdom will be an everlasting kingdom, and all rulers will worship and obey him."

Who does the Man of Lawlessness oppress? **the true saints of God.**

The fourth kingdom is Rome. It fell into ten kingdoms. The coming king that would rise would be different from the rest. It sounds like a spiritual power, since it will speak in place of God. It will be Roman and oppress the saints of God for 1,260 years. The placement of this information is the final warning that it is being held back by the present Roman Empire. The trumpets should lead to the fall of Rome and the appearance of the Man of Lawlessness.

Revelation, chapter thirteen, identifies two beasts; the two faces of the same entity. One is the political side, or face, that is revealed. The second is the spiritual side and its power that this entity will have. It would control and deceive for 1,260 years as predicted. This entity would survive to our day. However, it will be without its former power; only a shadow will exist.

---

[10] Chrysostom, Homily IV, 1

REVELATION 8:6
The Seven Trumpets

Revelation 8:6: "Then the seven angels who had the seven trumpets prepared to sound them."

We left off with the Roman Empire having the first four horsemen describing the Empire's coming history. The 5th seal described the last worldwide Roman persecution of Christians. The 6th seal, Christianity becomes the Empire's religion. The seven trumpets sound, but remember the chapter before stating: "After this I saw four angels standing at the four corners of the earth, holding back the four winds of the earth to prevent any wind from blowing on the land or on the sea or on any tree."

The use of four winds here indicates that four judgments are coming against Rome. The first four trumpets are grouped together just like the first four seals. The Man of Lawlessness is about to appear. Being on the other side of Rome's fall, we have the advantage of seeing what actually happened. We know the date of Rome's demise and the date of the rise of the next power that would last 1,260 years. Do Scripture and history align showing the sovereign control of God by His master plan? That is the purpose of reading Revelation in the manner chosen, from start to finish, sequentially; the same way history actually took place. Revelation is a roadmap of the **TRUE CHURCH'S HISTORY.** We now know that there will be a false church that will speak as if it was the true church. It is given 1,260 years to deceive.

REVELATION 8:7
The 1st Trumpet

"The first angel sounded his trumpet, and there came hail and fire mixed with blood, and it was hurled down upon the earth. A third of the earth was burned up, a third of the trees were burned up, and all the green grass was burned up."

CLUE: Rev 8:7

What is burned up? **Earth, Trees, and Grass**

The first angel sounded his trumpet and there came? **Hail and Fire**

What happens? **one third of the earth is affected** – trees and green grass are burned

Hail is the symbol of **God's judgment** (Job38: 22-23), and the combination of hail and fire (or thunderbolts) is similar to the plagues of Egypt (Exodus: 23; Psalms 18:13; 78:48; 10:32). Rome had not lost a major battle in centuries. Rome saw minor defeats as temporary setbacks. They would eventually conquer their foes and attain their prize. Inside their Empire, they ruled with iron teeth and crushed any opposition as shown with the Jews in Judea. It was now to change. God had decreed it.

HISTORICAL FULFILLMENT:

The first revelation is that Rome's Western Empire is now clearly seen as the subject of the first four trumpets. Recorded history reveals that God was judging one-third of the Roman Empire first.

The Battle of Hadrianople in 378 A.D. was a clarion call that times were changing. This battle marked the first time that a Roman army was decisively and completely defeated by an invader inside the Empire's borders. Roman Emperor Valens was even killed in the battle. Rome had not had to deal with invaders for eight hundred years. Rome even withdrew out of Great Britain to reinforce its northern borders.

Gibbon writes of "the tremendous sound of the Gothic trumpet." The Goths attack Gaul, Spain, and Italy from the north. The Goths are easily matched to the first trumpet. Scripture states that trees and green grass would be burned up. Gibbon records in his histories that the Goths did exactly that. Listen to the description by Gibbon: "Blood and conflagration and the burning of trees and herbage mark their path." The Goths from 408 – 410 A.D led by Alaric, sacked Rome. It was Alaric's policy to **burn orchards and vineyards, fill cultivated fields with stones, and generally destroy agriculture**. The fraction one-third has been explained as referring to Rome, who controlled one-third of the world. Therefore, one-third of the Roman Empire was under siege. The first blow came from the Goths. The second trumpet blows.

REVELATION 8:8-9
The 2nd Trumpet

"The second angel sounded his trumpet, and something like a huge mountain, all ablaze, was thrown into the sea. A third of the sea turned into blood, a third of the living creatures in the sea died, and a third of the ships were destroyed."

CLUE: Rev 8:8-9

A mountain is thrown ablaze into the sea. What is affected? **One third of the sea** turns to blood, **one-third die**, and **one third of the ships** are destroyed.

The second angel sounded his trumpet and there came? a mountain, all ablaze is thrown **into the sea**. The next battles appear to affect Rome in the sea.

What happens? One third of the **earth is affected**, one third of the **sea turns to blood**, and a third of the **ships are destroyed**.

HISTORICAL FULFILLMENT:

Rome's mastery of the sea had not been challenged for over six centuries. The Vandels, led by King Geneseric, crossed the Mediterranean, reached and rebuilt Carthage by 429 A.D. Historians refer to King Geneseric as the "Tyrant of the Sea." Barnes records that for the next thirty years they went about "destroying the ships and commerce of the Romans, and were distinguished in the downfall of the empire by their ravages on the islands and the sea." As Roman ships were sunk, the Tyrant of the Sea, who turned the seas red with the blood of Romans, slaughtered their mariners. In 455 A.D., they plundered Rome for fifteen days and filled the ships full of what was once the glory of Rome! The third trumpet sounds another blow.

REVELATION 8:10-11
The 3rd Trumpet

"The third angel sounded his trumpet, and a great star, blazing like a torch, fell from the sky on a third of the rivers and on the springs of water - the name of the star is Wormwood. A third of the waters turned bitter, and many people died from the waters that had become bitter."

CLUE: Rev 8:10-11

A great star falls. What happens?
One third of the rivers and springs turn bitter and many die.

The third angel sounded his trumpet and there came? **a great star** (person or enemy that blazes like a torch. A torch blazes bright but only for a short time).

HISTORICAL FULFILLMENT:

History shows a star did rise up as a torch and then disappear suddenly never to be heard of again. The star, as revealed in history, was "Attila the Hun." He was referred to as "the scourge of God." The Romans knew little of the Huns prior to 440 A.D. According to Gibbon's histories detailing the accounts of the Huns, they fought all their battles on rivers. Their strategy was to lure the Roman armies into crossing the river after they faked a retreat. Attila, with an 800,000 strong army decimated the regions of the Rhine, upper Danube, and Po rivers. In the Italian Alps, they shed so much blood, the rivers and springs that fed Europe's drinking water became polluted. Some historians of that time period have estimated that over 300,000 men lay slaughtered in the rivers. Attila took Rome and took the princess to be his wife. However, the torch only has a short life and Attila died on his wedding night. Attila and the Huns then disappear from history. We see that Rome's Western Empire history exactly matches the Scriptures. Notice that there is no need to twist history to match Scripture or vice versa. The simple reading of Scripture clearly matches history. It just fits. Time is up for Rome and its Western Empire. The fourth trumpet now blows.

REVELATION 8:11-13
The 4th Trumpet

"The fourth angel sounded his trumpet, and a third of the sun was struck, a third of the moon, and a third of the stars, so that a third of them turned dark. A third of the day was without light, and also a third of the night. As I watched, I heard an eagle that was flying in midair call out in a loud voice: 'Woe! Woe! Woe to the inhabitants of the earth, because of the trumpet blasts about to be sounded by the other three angels!'"

CLUE: Rev 8:11-13

A third of all lights go dark. This means that time is up for Rome.

What happens? **the sun, moon, and stars** were turned dark. An eagle announces what? Three woes are about to come upon the earth.

The sun, the moon, and the stars represent "the political firmament of Rome." Scripture indicates things are going to turn dark.

HISTORICAL FULFILLMENT:

No better description could have been predicted by the Apostle John back in 95 A.D. of what would happen in the year 476 A.D. The final emperor, Romulus-Augustus, was defeated and with his defeat came the end of imperial rule by Rome. Heruli under the command of Odoacer had won the battle and a barbarian king became the king of Rome. From that day, most historians date the beginning of what is known as the **"DARK AGES."** It ended civilization in the West. Their education system, roads, culture, and commerce would fall into chaos and remain fractured for over a thousand years. Systematic learning would not be rediscovered in the West until the Renaissance of the 1500's. One-third of the original Roman Empire, **the western division fell** to barbarians and now, for the first time, the Man of Lawlessness can appear, since Rome is free of the Empire who was restraining the appearance. Scripture focuses back on the other two-thirds of Rome. The fifth trumpet sounds, it is also called the 1st Woe. Here we see one revelation that will impact in two ways the people of the earth.

REVELATION 9:1-12
The 5th Trumpet (1ˢᵗ Woe)

"The fifth angel sounded his trumpet, and I saw a star that had fallen from the sky to the earth. The star was given the key to the shaft of the Abyss. When he opened the Abyss, smoke rose from it like the smoke from a gigantic furnace. The sun and sky were darkened by the smoke from the Abyss. And out of the smoke locusts came down upon the earth and were given power like that of scorpions of the earth. They were told not to harm the grass of the earth or any plant or tree, but only those people who did not have the seal of God on their foreheads. They were not given power to kill them, but only to torture them for five months. And the agony they suffered was like that of the sting of a scorpion when it strikes a man. During those days men will seek death, but will not find it; they will long to die, but death will elude them. The locusts looked like horses prepared for battle. On their heads they wore something like crowns of gold, and their faces resembled human faces. Their hair was like women's hair, and their teeth were like lions' teeth. They had breastplates like breastplates of iron, and the sound of their wings was like the thundering of many horses and chariots rushing into battle. They had tails and stings like scorpions, and in their tails they had power to torment people for five months. They had as king over them the angel of the Abyss, whose name in Hebrew is Abaddon, and in Greek, Apollyon. The first woe is past; two other woes are yet to come."

CLUES: Rev 9:1-12

A star that has fallen from the sky usually indicates what? **A person or enemy**
This star (person or enemy) has a key to what? **The abyss**
They are described as? **Locusts**
What will they not harm? **Grass or plants**
They have power to torture for? **Five months or 150 days**
Their hair was like? **Woman's hair**
This is what judgment? **The 5ᵗʰ Trumpet and 1ˢᵗ Woe**

What falls and is given a key to the Abyss? **A star**, indicating a person or enemy
What happens when the abyss is opened? The sun and sky are **darkened**
Out of the smoke or darkness comes what? **Locusts**

What are they told to do? **Harm no grass, plant, or tree** They do not use "**the slash and burn**" technique as the Goths had done.

How long will they be given power to kill? Five months and, in the biblical mindset, this would equal thirty days a month for five months or 150 total days. Applying the year for day rule it could be a period of **150 years** that this next star will have the power to **kill** (conquer) and **torment**.

The key to interpretation is to look at history and Scripture to find what fits easily, simply, and is an obvious match. It means looking at all possibilities and then picking the one that requires no massaging in order for it to be seen as matching the predicted prophecy. Using the clues from Scripture we are looking for a Star: a person who is famous, yet fallen. Second, they will have a darkened belief system, which will be the antithesis of God's truth, seen as light. Third, they are identified as "Locusts." Fourth, they will do no harm to grass, plants, or trees. Fifth, they will have 150 days or 150 years of power or conquest, where they kill and torture.

History reveals that the southern one-third of the Roman Empire fell to the Arabs during the Rise of Islam. We know Rome is impacted. Therefore, this appears to be the obvious match.

HISTORICAL FULFILLMENT:

"A star is fallen from Heaven" is a symbol for a prince who has been degraded and deprived of his rank. **Mohammed would have been a prince,** except his family in the previous generation lost their power.

Locusts represent the Saracens (Muslim Arabs) and their wars against the Roman Empire. Their campaigns started in 612 A.D. In biblical times, actual locust plagues often came from Arabia. For the Hebrew and Greek mind of the first century, this would be the logical conclusion; **Locusts meant Arabs.**

History shows that Mohammed's instruction in the Koran helps to pinpoint the Saracen (Arabs) as the people that the fifth trumpet prophecy identifies. **"Destroy no palm trees, nor any fields of corn, cut down no fruit trees."** This makes it easy to see the Arab-Muslims as the ones that Apostle John is naming.

Even a small detail like hair, the Apostle John uses as a key to ensure who is meant. They have faces like men and hair like women's hair. Like the Jews, but unlike the Romans and Greeks, the Arabs wore beards (the face of a man). Yet, it was well documented that they

> ## FULFILLMENT (Cont.)
>
> wore **long hair like women.** Pliny wrote of the "turbaned Arabs with their **uncut hair**." It was wrapped up and covered by their turban (crown).
>
> The 150 days is easily seen as 150 years since we have the luxury of being on this side of fulfillment. It was one hundred and fifty years from when Islam started their campaigns against the Empire in 612 A.D. and ended in 763 A.D. They were defeated at Tours by Charles Martel in 732. However, they continued to torture until 763 A.D. They had a policy known as **"Conversion by the Sword."** It was a real simple policy: you converted and praised Allah, or you got the sword. Their period of torment and conquest was over in 763 when they ended their policy of conversion by the sword and moved their capital to Baghdad on the Tigris River. Mohammed's name carries an interesting symbolic meaning in both Hebrew and Greek. It means **"Destroyer."** Here it is the 21st Century and Islamic nations are still lands where the light of the Gospel cannot be preached. They are lands where those in power use coercion to keep the faithful in line and in darkness. They still believe Islam can be spread by 'jihad' or Holy war. Spiritual darkness is upon the Islamic nations as the Apostle John predicted. The light of the Gospel and God's truth is not welcome. It is true in every detail exactly as the Apostle John predicted. It came from the abyss and has darkened minds for centuries.

Biederwolf clearly makes the point that history and Scripture match so that even a staunch opponent can see: "That there is a remarkable parallelism between this prediction and the rise and progress of the Mohammedan power the candid student must admit. Even Kelly, a staunch futurist, admits the interpretation to be well founded."

Two-thirds of Rome have fallen!

REVELATION 9:13-21
The 6th Trumpet (2ⁿᵈ Woe)

"The sixth angel sounded his trumpet, and I heard a voice coming from the horns of the golden altar that is before God. It said to the sixth angel who had the trumpet, 'Release the four angels who are bound at the great river Euphrates.' And the four angels who had been kept ready for this very hour and day and month and year were released to kill a third of mankind. The number of the mounted troops was two hundred million. I heard their number. The horses and riders I saw in my vision looked like this: Their breastplates were fiery red, dark blue, and yellow as sulfur. The heads of the horses resembled the heads of lions, and out of their mouths came fire, smoke and sulfur. A third of mankind was killed by the three plagues of fire, smoke and sulfur that came out of their mouths. The power of the horses was in their mouths and in their tails; for their tails were like snakes, having heads with which they inflict injury. The rest of mankind that were not killed by these plagues still did not repent of the work of their hands; they did not stop worshiping demons, and idols of gold, silver, bronze, stone and wood—idols that cannot see or hear or walk. Nor did they repent of their murders, their magic arts, their sexual immorality or their thefts."

CLUES: Rev 9:13-21

What is released? **Four angels who were bound**
Where were they bound? **The Euphrates River**
How long will they be kept back? **An hour and day and month and year**
What happens when they are released? **They kill one third**
What is the quantity of mounted troops? **200 million**
What are their colors? **Fiery red, dark blue, and sulfur yellow**

The sixth angel sounds his trumpet and destruction comes from the direction of the **Euphrates River**. How long until Rome's final third falls? Four angels are released **one year, one month, one day and, one hour; when totaled, equals 365 + 30 + 1 + 1/24 of a year. This is 396 years based on day to year principle.** We have our clues. We know the final one-third of the Roman Empire is to fall. The Eastern Empire is all that is left. The conquerors will come from the Euphrates River and they are horsemen (mounted troops).

They had red, blue, and yellow as their colors.

HISTORICAL FULFILLMENT:

The third of the Roman Empire that was left is the Grecian portion of what in history became the Byzantine Empire, with its capital at Constantinople. The Tartars, a warlike and numerous people, moved into the eastern banks of the Euphrates just before 1000 A.D. Under the leadership of Togrul, the Turkmans conquered Baghdad in 1055 A.D. and they converted to the Islamic religion. They were a warlike people and they quickly subjugated all of Persia and India. It would have been natural for the Turks to continue westward and attack the last vestiges of Rome. However, they seem bound by the Euphrates, as the Scripture states. It was not until 1056 that the Turks cross the Euphrates. Scripture indicates that the final third of the original Roman Empire would not fall for 396 – 397 years. The Turks begin their assault and it takes the 396 years for them to conquer and take Constantinople, bringing an end to the final one-third as Scripture predicted. The Turks, by this time, are known as the Ottoman Empire. The old Rome is now gone.

What is meant by the Two Hundred Million? Elliott helps to clarify from historical records that Tartars and Turks used the term "myriads" in numbering their troops. The term can be translated "two myriad myriads." This refers to an indefinite number.

The colors of the Turks, which became the Ottoman Empire are and have always been scarlet, blue, and yellow.

The question I had was why it took until 1453 A.D. for the Turks, the world's greatest empire by the mid Fifteenth Century, to subdue Constantinople. The answer will come later, but it has to do with a mass exodus of their Christian scholars to Western Europe just prior to the Reformation. When you look at history in light of what God was doing, the holding back appears to be for a reason. Europe, prior to this time, was not fertile ground for Christian scholars as you will see following.

THE REVIVED ROMAN POWER

Revelation Chapters 10-19 is a battle between the rider of a white horse who is called **Faithful and True;** on his robe and on his thigh he has this name written: **KING OF KINGS AND LORD OF LORDS** – this is obviously Jesus Christ. The opposition is a woman sitting on a scarlet **beast** that was covered with blasphemous names and had seven heads and ten horns. The woman was dressed in purple and scarlet, and was glittering with gold, precious stones, and pearls. She held a golden cup in her hand, filled with abominable things and the filth of her adulteries. This title was written on her forehead: **MYSTERY BABYLON THE GREAT, THE MOTHER OF PROSTITUTES AND OF THE ABOMINATIONS OF THE EARTH.** The woman was drunk with the **blood of the saints**, the blood of those who bore testimony to Jesus. This beast is the antithesis of all that for which Jesus Christ stands. It is the ultimate example of false religion, known as the Mystery of Babylon. She was drunk on the blood of the saints of God. This false religion will slay God's true followers in mass and for 1,260 years, according to prophecy.

We now turn to history to see who this could be. Our point of reference is after the Beast has had its power and influence reduced. We currently know the Catholic Church as a post-Vatican II church. Today, the Vatican Church is a mere shadow of its former reach and control. God is clearly targeting the Papacy, the Vatican, and its insidious hierarchy. In 1964, the Pope and the Vatican were forced under extreme pressure to put an end to many of the "mysteries." The "Declaration on Religious Freedom" of Vatican II is a virtual death warrant to the Papacy – signed, sealed, and delivered by the Pope himself. Today the Catholic Church really has two separate parts in struggle. One is the local priests and their people, who continue to want more freedom and truth from the Scriptures taught. This is why the Catholic Church has many re-born Catholics. God sees only Christians, His children. We are unified in Christ in spite of our theological differences. The second part of the Catholic Church is the unrepentant hierarchy, whom God has asked to repent. This terrible history is now our combined saga of the war for spiritual freedom, shared by both Protestants and Catholics. It is a time (1,260 years) when the Papacy would chase true believers. They survived only to bring the Good News to both Catholics and Protestants of our day.

REVELATION 10
The Angel and the Little Scroll [Book]

Revelation 10, "When I saw another mighty angel coming down from heaven. He was robed in a cloud, with a rainbow above his head; his face was like the sun, and his legs were like fiery pillars. He was holding a little scroll [book], which lay open in his hand. He planted his right foot on the sea and his left foot on the land, and he gave a loud shout like the roar of a lion. When he shouted, the voices of the seven thunders spoke. And when the seven thunders spoke, I was about to write; but I heard a voice from heaven say, 'Seal up what the seven thunders have said and do not write it down.' Then the angel I had seen standing on the sea and on the land raised his right hand to heaven. And he swore by him who lives for ever and ever, who created the heavens and all that is in them, the earth and all that is in it, and the sea and all that is in it, and said, 'There will be no more delay! But in the days when the seventh angel is about to sound his trumpet, the mystery of God will be accomplished, just as he announced to his servants the prophets.' Then the voice that I had heard from heaven spoke to me once more: 'Go, take the scroll that lies open in the hand of the angel who is standing on the sea and on the land.' So I went to the angel and asked him to give me the little scroll. He said to me, 'Take it and eat it. It will turn your stomach sour, but in your mouth it will be as sweet as honey.' I took the little scroll from the angel's hand and ate it. It tasted as sweet as honey in my mouth, but when I had eaten it, my stomach turned sour. Then I was told, 'You must prophesy again about many peoples, nations, languages and kings.'"

CLUES: Rev 10

What is opened? **A book (scroll)**
When? **Now, no more delay**
How will it taste? **Sweet, but sour later**
What starts? **Preaching**

Revelation, Chapter 10 is about a book that is to be opened. Looking to history, we know the **Book is the Bible**. We know from history that the Bible was hand-copied (limited distribution) and it was not in the language of common people. This was to change, according to the announcement by the angel.

The second thing that stands out is there is **no more delay**. When should this happen? The process should begin immediately.

The open book will turn sour in your stomach but will be honey in your mouth. They eat the Bible that has become open and available, but it will be sour in the stomach. This indicates that knowing the truth of the Bible will come at a cost.

The final key is the last sentence, **"You must prophesy again about many peoples, nations, languages, and kings."**

Where are we in history? The last chapter ended in 1453 A.D with the fall of Constantinople. The time frame to look for fulfillment would be starting in the mid Fifteenth Century (1400's and on) and extending, based on what history reveals about the Bible being opened to people.

HISTORICAL FULFILLMENT:

History reveals that two developments were of critical importance at this time. The first was the migration of many Greek scholars to Western Europe. The second was the invention of the moveable type printing known as the Guttenberg Press around 1455. The Greek language was taught starting in 1458; printing of the Greek New Testament by Eramus in the year 1516; printing of the first Swiss New Testament by Zwingli in the year 1518; printing of the first German New Testament by Luther in 1522; printing of the first English and Swedish Bibles by Tyndale in 1526; printing in Italian in the year 1532; printing of the Danish Bible in 1537; the Great Bible commanded to be placed in every English church in 1539. The most well known Bible started printing in 1611 – the King James Version. As we see, there was an explosion or opening of the Bible to many people that started as predicted by Scripture and continues to this day.

How does knowing the word of God, which is sweet as honey, become sour in their stomachs? The Protestant movement met the full fury of the Roman Catholic Church. In 1478, the Papacy began the Spanish Inquisition, wiping out virtually all Protestants in that nation by 1558. In 1572, on St. Bartholomew's Day, the Catholic Church slaughtered up to 50,000 Protestants in one day. In France, the French Protestants, known as the Huguenots, met severe opposition ending in a civil war that was halted only after the Pope issued the Edict of Toleration in 1598. This was just a part of the price that was paid by those who ate of the book. The Holy Roman Church was drunk on the blood of the saints of God. H. Gratten Guinness states: **"It has been calculated that the Popes have, directly or indirectly, slain on account of their faith fifty-millions of martyrs."** The Church of Rome has shed more innocent Christian blood than any other institution in history. No

FULFILLMENT (Cont.):

historian would dispute this fact of history. History again matches what Revelation describes would happen.

A Catholic clergyman named John Wycliffe would begin to see that the Scriptures should be the property of all people. He decided to translate the whole Bible from Latin into English. He completed this around 1382, 150 years prior to the Reformation. He set out to plant the truth and His followers became known as the "Lollards," a derogatory term meaning "Idle Babblers." This translation infected England with the Truth. The Catholic Church acted against this heretical movement and, in a few decades, stomped out most of the effects of Wycliffe's work and drove his followers underground. In 1425, the Catholic Church, hoping to send a message to those who were thinking of committing treachery against the Holy Roman Church, ordered Wycliffe's bones exhumed and burned along with some two hundred books he had written. The seed planted would come back to haunt the Catholic Church. Like any movement for truth or freedom, driving it underground never really ends the issue.

Again, this is recorded history. It was a time when the Catholic Church was different than it is today. It fulfilled prophecy. The goal is to match Revelation to history. We see that they match, which shows God's Word and history align perfectly.

The Protestants would **prophesy (preach)** God's Word.
Barnes notes: "preaching was a thing comparatively little known before many ages. The grand business in the papal communion was not, and is not, preaching, but the performance of rites and ceremonies. Genuflections, crossings, burning of incense, processions, music, constitute the characteristic features of all papal churches; the grand thing that distinguishes the Protestant churches all over the world, just in proportion as they are Protestant, **is preaching.**" Here we see that a simple and clear reading of Revelation shows a continued match between prophecy and historical fulfillment.
Preaching started right on time.

REVELATION 11:1-14
The Two Witnesses

"I was given a reed like a measuring rod and was told, 'Go and measure the temple of God and the altar, and count the worshipers there. But exclude the outer court; do not measure it, because it has been given to the Gentiles. They will trample on the holy city for 42 months. And I will give power to my two witnesses, and they will prophesy for 1,260 days, clothed in sackcloth.' These are the two olive trees and the two lampstands that stand before the Lord of the earth. If anyone tries to harm them, fire comes from their mouths and devours their enemies. This is how anyone who wants to harm them must die. These men have power to shut up the sky so that it will not rain during the time they are prophesying; and they have power to turn the waters into blood and to strike the earth with every kind of plague as often as they want. When they have finished their testimony, the beast that comes up from the Abyss will attack them, and overpower and kill them. Their bodies will lie in the street of the great city, which is figuratively called Sodom and Egypt, where also their Lord was crucified.

For three and a half days men from every people, tribe, language, and nation will gaze on their bodies and refuse them burial. The inhabitants of the earth will gloat over them and will celebrate by sending each other gifts, because these two prophets had tormented those who live on the earth. But after the three and a half days a breath of life from God entered them, and they stood on their feet, and terror struck those who saw them. Then they heard a loud voice from heaven saying to them, 'Come up here.' And they went up to heaven in a cloud, while their enemies looked on. At that very hour there was a severe earthquake and a tenth of the city collapsed. Seven thousand people were killed in the earthquake, and the survivors were terrified and gave glory to the God of heaven. The second woe has passed; the third woe is coming soon."

The Final Trumpet

> ## CLUES: Rev 11:1-14
>
> What is a measuring rod? **A standard by which to judge**
> How long trampled? **42 months, or 1,260 days or 1,260 years (a year for a day principle applied)**
> The two witnesses have? **Power**
> How long is preaching in a sackcloth? **1,260 days or 1,260 years**
> The preaching ones do what to the beast? **Turn the waters into blood and strike the earth with every kind of plague**
> How long are the bodies dead? **Three and one half days or three and one half years**
> What do the victors do? **Celebrate and gloat!**
> What happened after three and a half days to bring terror to those of the beast? **God breathes life into them!**
> What happened due to the severe earthquake? **One tenth collapsed and 7000 are killed**
> What then? **They testified and gave Glory to God**

The temple of God throughout the New Testament is always viewed as the Church. John is to measure the temple (church), the altar (sacrifice), and those who worship there (membership). The standard is the Word of God. How does the Word of God say we are paid for? What is the sacrifice that was made? Jesus the Lamb of God was the sacrifice who died for us. The final question is what makes one a child of God? What determines membership? This is the point of having a standard to judge the Holy Roman Church. History reveals that the Reformation was exactly about measuring the Word of God to the traditions and doctrines of the Papacy.

We know from history that the true church was persecuted. The fire comes out of their mouths and devours their enemies. The word spoken by Christians exposes the bankrupt traditions of any false teaching and reveals our sinful lives. Who were the **Two Witnesses?** These are the same Two Witnesses the church has had since the Apostle John finished the Bible. The two witnesses are the **Old and New Testaments.** They will be the two witnesses given to the true church right up until Christ at His second coming. The 1,260 years represent the time given to the Holy Roman Church to repent, at which time God will reduce their hold and power. History shows that, as the Papacy inflicted death on the heretics (true believers), the Catholic Church suffered all kinds of plagues. Listen to Elliott as he identified the judgments as "bloodshed of wars inflicted in God's providence on the enemies of the witnesses." Caringola records that when Catholic nations like France and

Spain persecuted the true Christians, "there is recorded a continuous account of blood along the waterways of Europe." This is right in line with what Scripture declares, "they have power to turn the waters into blood and to strike the earth with every kind of plague as often as they want."

HISTORICAL FULFILLMENT:
The Defeat of the Witnesses by the Beast

Pope Innocent III in the 12th Century tried to exterminate every trace of resistance to Papal authority in Europe. At the Third Lateran Council of 1179, war was declared on all heretics. The Inquisitions started in 1231. Scripture predicts that their dead bodies would not be allowed to be buried. History bears this sad fact as being fulfilled by the Holy Roman Church. The denial of burial was reconfirmed by multiple councils and by decree of many Popes. Wycliff's body was exhumed and burned; Huss was reduced to ashes and tossed into Lake Geneva. A papal bull was issued in 1513 calling the remaining Bohemian brethren to present their cause before the Fifth Lateran Council. No one appeared. At the end of the council on May 5, 1514, Elliott writes,

"The orator of the session ascended the pulpit; and, amidst the applause of the assembled council, uttered that memorable exclamation which…was never, I believe, pronounced before, and certainly never since – '*I am nemo reclamat, nullus obsistit*' – 'There is an end of resistance to the Papal rule and religion; opposers there exist no more;' and again. 'The whole body of Christendom is now seen to be subjected to its Head [the Pope].'"

The Pope had a great festival to celebrate the death of the two witnesses. Has the Pope defeated God's Two Witnesses? Not Exactly!

HISTORICAL FULFILLMENT: THE TWO WITNESSES STOOD UP

God raises them up after three and one half days. This means three and one half years from **May 5, 1514**, the two witnesses would rise and be noticed. The two witnesses are the Old and New Testaments, which represent the only divinely revealed books and truth from God. The Pope had declared victory. God's Word indicates that the truth of the Bible would be reasserted three and a half years later. Additionally, Scripture infers that the papacy will feel great fear.

THREE AND ONE HALF YEARS LATER
ON OCTOBER 31st 1517,
LUTHER NAILED THE 95 THESES TO THE DOOR OF THE WITTENBURG CHURCH!
THEY STOOD UP!

Luther's 95 Theses were an indictment of the Holy Roman Catholic Church, declaring that its doctrines and traditions did not agree with the Bible (the Two Witnesses). How did Pope Hadrian react? "The heretics Huss and Jerome seem now to be **alive again** in the person of Luther." What the Catholic Church thought had been destroyed only went underground. Scripture predicts additional resistance along with a severe earthquake, indicating a political impact to the Holy Roman Catholic Church's power base.

A great earthquake of political convulsions followed this. Two consequences fall on the papacy. Scripture reveals a tenth, indicating only a partial, reduction of their papal empire. This partial reduction was when **the Church of England declared itself independent in 1529**, making England the first nation ever to break away from the Pope's strong grips. The second consequence is seven thousand men were killed. History shows that seven other entities (countries or provinces) broke from under the Pope's domination at this time. They were Holland, Zealand, Utrecht, Frieseland, Groningen, Overyssel, and Gutherland.
The second woe has passed.
The third woe is soon coming.

REVELATION 11:15-19
The Seventh Trumpet

"The seventh angel sounded his trumpet, and there were loud voices in heaven, which said: 'The kingdom of the world has become the kingdom of our Lord and of his Christ, and he will reign for ever and ever.' And the twenty-four elders, who were seated on their thrones before God, fell on their faces and worshiped God, saying: 'We give thanks to you, Lord God Almighty, the One who is and who was, because you have taken your great power and have begun to reign. The nations were angry; and your wrath has come. The time has come for judging the dead, and for rewarding your servants the prophets and your saints and those who reverence your name, both small and great - and for destroying those who destroy the earth.' Then God's temple in heaven was opened, and within his temple was seen the ark of his covenant. And there came flashes of lightning, rumblings, peals of thunder, an earthquake and a great hailstorm."

The seventh trumpet sounds and it brings major changes for the Holy Roman Church. It is the start of the pouring out of God's wrath upon the Papacy. The temple of God (we know represents the Church) appears to be given an open door (opportunity) and is empowered to overcome all who stand in Her way. In the Old Testament, the Ark was placed in front of the Israelite army and it literally destroyed the enemies of the Israelites. This section ends with things being under siege by God and His people. History does bear out the impact of the Reformation and the almost complete destruction of the Holy Roman Church.

Chapters 4-11 are concerned mainly with the outward state of the church. This deals with the secular and political developments impacting the church. Chapters 12-19 contain a second set of visions that cover the same time frame, except dealing with the internal affairs of the church. Both the false church and the faithful church are revealed with reference to their relationship to each other. Before we move to the next section, let's do a quick review of what has been fulfilled in history to this point in accordance with Revelation.

QUICK REVIEW

In Revelation we have covered the following so far:

Chapter 1 - Prologue, Greetings, and Doxology; the Apostle John is instructed to write down what he will see and send it to the Churches.

Chapter 2 - Church of **Ephesus** warned for forsaking first love. Those who overcome will eat of the Tree of Life. Church of **Smyrna** receives no warning, called spiritually rich. Those who overcome will not suffer the second death. Church of **Pergamum** warned about holding to wrong teachings. Those who overcome will receive a white stone. Church in **Thyatria** was following teachings of Jezebel. Those who overcome receive authority over all nations.

Chapter 3 - Church of **Sardis** told that they are spiritually dead. Those who overcome will be dressed in white and their names are in the Book of Life. Church in **Philadelphia** has an open door given to them. Those who overcome will receive a crown. Church of **Laodicea** is wealthy, but in reality is wretched.

Chapter 4 - The apostle John is taken to the throne in heaven.

Chapter 5 - The Scroll containing the seals is opened by the Lamb of God.

Chapter 6 - The Seals are opened:

> *1st SEAL* - The White Horse - The Peace of Rome (98 -180 A.D) Rome is victorious and expanded
>
> *2nd SEAL* - The Red Horse - Eighty Emperors in ninety years of Civil War (180 - 270 A.D.)
>
> *3rd SEAL* - The Black Horse – Era of taxation, famines, and shortages, followed war
>
> *4th SEAL* - The Pale Horse - Death, plague and depopulation. (Ends 296 A.D)
>
> *5th SEAL* - The Era of the Martyrs; Christians suffer final worldwide persecution (303-313 A.D.)
>
> *6th SEAL* - Christianity is elevated to Empire's official religion; the Fall of Paganism and Rise of Christianity (313 - 460 A.D.)

Chapter 7 - The Sealing of the 144,000 firstfruits from the tribes of Israel; Apostle John sees the Great Multitude of saints that no one can count.

Chapters 8 & 9 - The Seventh Seal is opened and it has seven trumpets. The four winds (trumpets) blow against Rome, but wait until Christianity spread. Four northern invasions were fulfilled between 400 - 476 A.D.

> *1st TRUMPET* - The Goths led by Alaric I 410 A.D. sacked Rome.

2nd **TRUMPET** – "The Tyrant of the Sea" The Vandels led by King Geneseric in 429 - 455 A.D. plundered Rome. They destroy Roman sea power.

3rd **TRUMPET** - The rise of Attila the Hun in 440 A.D. "The Scourge of the Rivers"

4th **TRUMPET** - Rome falls in 476 A.D and enters the "Dark Ages." Civilization does not return until the 1500's.

5th **TRUMPET** –The rise of Mohammedanism starts the 150 years of conversion by the sword (612 – 763 A.D.). The second third of the Roman Empire falls.

6th **TRUMPET** – "The rise of the Turkish Empire" The Turks cross the Euphrates River and the last third of the old Roman Empire falls in 1453, when Constantinople is conquered.

Chapter 10 - The book will be opened; it tastes like honey, but turns sour. The Word of God is translated and printed in common languages.

Chapter 11- The Two Witnesses are clearly seen as the Old and New Testaments. They are the eternal witness given to man with the seal of God on it. The time that the Holy Roman Church has is 1,260 Years. The Papacy claimed victory over the true Christians (heretics) on May 5, 1514, only to be foiled exactly three and one half years later, on October 31, 1517, by Martin Luther with the posting of the 95 Theses on the door of the Wittenburg church.

The Final Trumpet

Visual Review of History and Revelation

Pre-95 A.D.	Seven Churches established
95 A.D.	Apostle John receives revelation and records it

Seals opened - Must Start Shortly - was as just 3 years 98 A.D.

98 - 180 A.D.	1st Seal - White Horse - Peace of Rome
180 - 270 A.D.	2nd Seal - Red Horse - Civil War (80 emperors)
~200 - 303 A.D.	3rd Seal - Black Horse - Shortages & Famine
~250 - 303 A.D.	4th Seal - Pale Horse - Plague & Depopulation
303 - 313 A.D.	5th Seal - Era of Martyrs - Last Worldwide Persecution
313 - 460 A.D.	6th Seal - Rise of the Christian Church

7th Seal opened which contains Seven Trumpets

410 A.D.	1st Trumpet - Goths lead by Alaric I sack Rome
429-455 A.D.	2nd Trumpet - King Geneseric - War at Sea
440 A.D.	3rd Trumpet - Attila the Hun - Rivers Turned Red
476 A.D.	4th Trumpet - Dark Ages Begin
612 A.D. & on	5th Trumpet - Rise of Islam - Conversion by Sword
1453 A.D	6th Trumpet - Rise of Turkish Empire - Last third falls

7th Trumpet delayed until Seven Plagues (bowls) Poured Out

THE BOOK IS OPENED - PREACHING STARTS REFORMATION

1455 A.D	Guttenberg Press
15-16th Centuries	Printing of Bibles In Common Languages
May 5, 1514	Papacy claims victory over heretics (true believers)
October 31, 1517	Luther nailed 95 Theses to the Wittenburg Church

REVELATION 12
The Woman and the Dragon

"A great and wondrous sign appeared in heaven: a woman clothed with the sun, with the moon under her feet and a crown of twelve stars on her head. She was pregnant and cried out in pain as she was about to give birth. Then another sign appeared in heaven: an enormous red dragon with seven heads and ten horns and seven crowns on his heads. His tail swept a third of the stars out of the sky and flung them to the earth. The dragon stood in front of the woman who was about to give birth, so that he might devour her child the moment it was born. She gave birth to a son, a male child, who will rule all the nations with an iron scepter. And her child was snatched up to God and to his throne. The woman fled into the desert to a place prepared for her by God, where she might be taken care of for 1,260 days. And there was war in heaven. Michael and his angels fought against the dragon, and the dragon and his angels fought back. But he was not strong enough, and they lost their place in heaven. The great dragon was hurled down - that ancient serpent called the devil, or Satan, who leads the whole world astray. He was hurled to the earth, and his angels with him. Then I heard a loud voice in heaven say: 'Now have come the salvation and the power and the kingdom of our God, and the authority of his Christ. For the accuser of our brothers, who accuses them before our God day and night, has been hurled down. They overcame him by the blood of the Lamb and by the word of their testimony; they did not love their lives so much as to shrink from death. Therefore rejoice, you heavens and you who dwell in them! But woe to the earth and the sea, because the devil has gone down to you! He is filled with fury, because he knows that his time is short.' When the dragon saw that he had been hurled to the earth, he pursued the woman who had given birth to the male child. The woman was given the two wings of a great eagle, so that she might fly to the place prepared for her in the desert, where she would be taken care of for a time, times and half a time, out of the serpent's reach. Then from his mouth the serpent spewed water like a river, to overtake the woman and sweep her away with the torrent. But the earth helped the woman by opening its mouth and swallowing the river that the dragon had spewed out of his mouth. Then the dragon was enraged at the woman and went off to make war against the rest of her offspring-those who obey God's commandments and hold to the testimony of Jesus. And the dragon stood on the shore of the sea."

This Chapter is to be read and understood in light of the totality of Scripture's message and what has transpired in history from a spiritual perspective. It opens with the woman (Israel, the twelve crowns or tribes) about to give birth. This refers to the coming of the Messiah. Then the red dragon appears with seven heads (indicates the seven hills of Rome) and His tail has conquered one third of the world. The dragon stood in front of the woman. We know in history that Rome conquered Palestine in 63 B.C. Now the red dragon (Rome) is in a position to devour the male child before He has a chance. This male child (Jesus Christ) was to rule all nations with an iron scepter. This simply implies the birth of Christ and that He will rule all nations one day. Satan knew the Messiah was coming. Did Satan attempt to kill Christ when he was only a child? Yes - this is an historical fact. Then the male child was taken to heaven to His throne. This is exactly what is recorded. Jesus was crucified, rose up, and ascended to His throne. The woman (originally Israel in the Old Testament, becomes the church in the New Testament) is to be persecuted for 1,260 days. This is exactly what happened in history.

The Christians started out on the day of Pentecost 120 strong. Christianity became the official religion of the Empire and then a period known as the Rise of Christianity expanded the church to new heights. However, God prepares a place of protection for the Church. Why? because war broke out in heaven and Satan with his angels are cast down onto the earth. Then we have an announcement in heaven: it tells us that the Kingdom of God has come; Satan is the accuser; the church has overcome by the Blood of the Lamb (Christ); Christians die for their testimony; and Satan knows his time is short. The church is given two wings (divine protection) for 1,260 years until the attack is done on the true church. This is recorded in history. It is historically recorded that the Holy Roman Catholic Church did chase the woman (true church) for 1,260 years. Again, this is a simple reading using the Scriptures, proper application of doctrine, and the facts of history. The next chapter will provide some more details about who Satan is going to use to do his corrupt work. It is the Beast of Revelation, as identified in Chapter 13. This beast has two sides: one political and the other spiritual.

REVELATION 13:1-12
The Beast out of the Sea

"And I saw a beast coming out of the sea. He had ten horns and seven heads, with ten crowns on his horns, and on each head a blasphemous name. The beast I saw resembled a leopard, but had feet like those of a bear and a mouth like that of a lion. The dragon [Satan] gave the beast his power and his throne and great authority. One of the heads of the beast seemed to have had a fatal wound, but the fatal wound had been healed. The whole world was astonished and followed the beast. Men worshiped the dragon because he had given authority to the beast, and they also worshiped the beast and asked, 'Who is like the beast? Who can make war against him?' The beast was given a mouth to utter proud words and blasphemies and to exercise his authority for forty-two months. He opened his mouth to blaspheme God, and to slander his name and his dwelling place and those who live in heaven. He was given power to make war against the saints and to conquer them. And he was given authority over every tribe, people, language and nation. All inhabitants of the earth will worship the beast - all whose names have not been written in the book of life belonging to the Lamb that was slain from the creation of the world. He, who has an ear, let him hear. If anyone is to go into captivity, into captivity he will go. If anyone is to be killed with the sword, with the sword he will be killed. This calls for patient endurance and faithfulness on the part of the saints."

The beast is the Holy Roman Catholic church. He had ten horns and seven heads. The seven heads always ties the beast to Rome. The ten horns will be explained below. Daniel, chapter seven, predicted and provided the interpretation and necessary clues to see who in history fulfills this prophecy. The dragon "Satan" gives the beast his power. Since Satan is the temporary ruler of the world, he can allow the Papacy to do his agenda. The Roman Empire, the fourth empire, would appear to have collapsed and receive its deathblow (a fatal wound). However, on the same seat rises the Holy Roman Catholic Church, again the length of power is 1,260 years (42 months). Three additional facts related to the beast are provided. First, he will blaspheme and slander God. Second, He will make war on the saints of God. Third, all inhabitants of this world who worship the beast will not have their names in the Book of Life. We will review Daniel 7:15-28 and glean from the Old Testament additional clarification.

DANIEL 7:15-28
The Interpretation of the Dream

"I, Daniel, was troubled in spirit, and the visions that passed through my mind disturbed me. I approached one of those standing there and asked him the true meaning of all this. So he told me and gave me the interpretation of these things: '**The four great beasts are four kingdoms that will rise from the earth.** [Babylon, Medo-Persia, Greece & Rome as detailed in Daniel Chapter 2:37-35] But the saints of the Most High will receive the kingdom and will possess it forever—yes, for ever and ever.' Then I wanted to know the true meaning of the fourth beast, which was different from all the others and most terrifying, with its iron teeth and bronze claws—the beast that crushed and devoured its victims and trampled underfoot whatever was left. I also wanted to know about the **ten horns** on its head and about the other horn that came up, before which **three** of them fell—**the horn that looked more imposing than the others and that had eyes and a mouth that spoke boastfully.** As I watched, this horn was waging war against the saints and defeating them, until the Ancient of Days came and pronounced judgment in favor of the saints of the Most High, and the time came when they possessed the kingdom.

He gave me this explanation: 'The fourth beast is a fourth kingdom that will appear on earth. It will be different from all the other kingdoms and will devour the whole earth, trampling it down and crushing it. **The ten horns are ten kings who will come from this kingdom.** [Rome fell into ten nations.] After them another king will arise, **different** from the earlier ones; **he will subdue three kings.** [Rome conquers these three kingdoms.] He will **speak against the Most High and oppress his saints** and **try to change the set times and the laws.** The saints will be handed over to him for a **time, times and half a time.** [1,260 years]

'But the court will sit, and his power will be taken away and completely destroyed forever. Then the sovereignty, power and greatness of the kingdoms under the whole heaven will be handed over to the saints, the people of the Most High. His kingdom will be an everlasting kingdom, and all rulers will worship and obey him.' This is the end of the matter. I, Daniel, was deeply troubled by my thoughts, and my face turned pale, but I kept the matter to myself."

HISTORICAL FULFILLMENT:

The ten kingdoms that Rome fell into were the Anglo-Saxons, the Franks, the Allmani, the Burgundians, the Visigoths, the Suevi, the Vandals, the Ostrogoths, the Bavarians, and the Lombards. The next Roman power would be different than the first. Rome was a political empire that conquered people and land; whereas, the Holy Roman Church took possession of land, people, and souls. The three kingdoms that the revived Rome (Holy Roman Church) would subdue were the Lombards, Vandels, and Ostrogoths, which are recorded in history. In 533 AD, the horn of the Vandels in Africa, Corisca and Sardinia was crushed. Justinian's forces, under Belisarius, routed the Ostrogoths in Italy. Pepin and Charlemagne eradicated the only other danger to the power base of the Holy Roman Catholic church. By the year 752 A.D., all three horns that posed a threat to the bishop of Rome had been destroyed. The Holy Roman Church would speak against God.

The church had many bishops in various dioceses and they were all considered equal. This was to change in 533 A.D. In that year a decree was issued by the eastern Emperor, Justinian, elevating the bishop of Rome as "head of all the holy Churches, and of all the holy priests of God."

The first pope was to be Boniface III. This starts the clock for the 1,260 years given to wear out the saints of God. The years 1793-94 will then be years that the power of the Holy Roman Church is reduced. Complete details will be provided later as Revelation gives us a list of clues.

The seeds of deception started back in 378 A.D. when the title of Pontifex Maximus – the official title for the high priest of the mysteries – was taken by the bishop of Rome. God immediately punished Rome because of this insidious act. Remember, earlier in 378 A.D. was the first time that a Roman army was soundly defeated and their Emperor also perished in the battle.

Did the Catholic Church speak against God? Turning to history we find out that it did. Blasphemy, according to the Bible, is defined as making oneself equal to God and claiming the power and authority to forgive sins. The popes have publicly, and in writing, made pronouncement of this claim for all to see.

FULFILLMENT (Cont.):

"The Roman Pontiff judges all men, but is judged by no one...I have the authority of the King of Kings. I am all in all and above all...wherefore, if those things that I do be said not to be done of man but of God, what can you call me but God?" No one can judge him. Only God is beyond judgment.

Listen as Pope Leo XIII in 1894 claimed, "We hold the place of Almighty God on earth." In 1922, Pope Pius X boasted, "You know I am the Holy Father, the representative of God on earth, the Vicar of Christ, which means I am God on the earth."

History reveals, as I shared earlier, that the Catholic Church has spilled more blood of Christians than any other entity on earth. Reading books like <u>Foxes' Book of Martyrs</u> or Guinness' <u>The Approaching End of the Age</u> will give you a glimpse into the battle. The final item that prophecy reveals to us is that the false Church will change the set times and laws.

The Holy Roman Catholic Church did exactly this in the 16th Century. The Gregorian calendar resulted from a perceived need to reform the method of calculating the dates of Easter. Under the Julian calendar, the dating of Easter had become standardized, using March 21 as the date of the equinox and the Metonic cycle as the basis for calculating lunar phases. By the Thirteenth Century, it was realized that the true equinox had regressed from March 21 (its supposed date at the time of the Council of Nicea, +325) to a date earlier in the month. As a result, Easter was drifting away from its springtime position and was losing its relation with the Jewish Passover. Over the next four hundred years, scholars debated the "correct" time for celebrating Easter. The Church made intermittent attempts to solve the Easter question, without reaching a consensus.

At the behest of the Council of Trent, Pope Pius V introduced a new Breviary in 1568 and Missal in 1570, both of which included adjustments to the lunar tables and the leap-year system. Pope Gregory XIII, who succeeded Pope Pius in 1572, soon convened a commission to consider reform of the calendar, since he considered his predecessor's measures inadequate. The papal bull "Inter Gravissimus" signed on February 24, 1582, instituted the recommendations of Pope Gregory's calendar commission.

FULFILLMENT (Cont.):

Ten days were deleted from the calendar, so October 4, 1582, was followed by October 15, 1582, thereby causing the vernal equinox of 1583 and subsequent years to occur about March 21. A new table of New Moons and Full Moons was introduced for determining the date of Easter. Subject to the logistical problems of communication and governance in the 16th Century, the new calendar was promulgated through the Roman-Catholic world.

Protestant states initially rejected the calendar, but gradually accepted it over the coming centuries. The Eastern Orthodox churches rejected the new calendar and continued to use the Julian calendar with traditional lunar tables for calculating Easter. Because the purpose of the Gregorian calendar was to regulate the cycle of Christian holidays, its acceptance in the non-Christian world was initially not at issue. But as international communications developed, the civil rules of the Gregorian calendar were gradually adopted around the world. The Holy Roman Catholic Church set Christmas based on the winter solstice, a pagan holiday worshipping the sun. As you can see, the calendar was changed and there was to be the mixing of Christian concepts, theology, laws, and dates with the pagan belief system known as the "Mystery of Babylon," except it would have Christian terminology.

The Beast from the Sea is the Holy Roman Catholic Church in all its political power and glory. It conquers, wages wars, changes the calendars, and even declares itself God. Yet, another beast shall rise. It is the other side or face the beast wants to present. The Beast of the Earth we see demonstrates that deception is taken to new heights! The Beast of the Sea and the Beast of the Earth are one.

REVELATION 13:11-18
The Beast out of the Earth

"Then I saw another beast, coming out of the earth. He had two horns like a lamb, but he spoke like a dragon. He exercised all the authority of the first beast on his behalf, and made the earth and its inhabitants worship the first beast, whose fatal wound had been healed. And he performed great and miraculous signs, even causing fire to come down from heaven to earth in full view of men. Because of the signs he was given power to do on behalf of the first beast, he deceived the inhabitants of the earth. He ordered them to set up an image in honor of the beast that was wounded by the sword and yet lived. He was given power to give breath to the image of the first beast, so that it could speak and cause all who refused to worship the image to be killed. He also forced everyone, small and great, rich and poor, free and slave, to receive a mark on his right hand or on his forehead, so that no one could buy or sell unless he had the mark, which is the name of the beast or the number of his name. This calls for wisdom. If anyone has insight, let him calculate the number of the beast, for it is man's number. His number is 666."

CLUES: Rev 13:11-18

This beast had two horns like a lamb, but spoke like? **A Dragon [Satan]**
They will do great and miraculous signs.
Power is given to the image and all who refuse to worship, or pay homage, are to be killed. Who is the image that demanded absolute worship in history? He will force all to take the **mark of the beast** if they want to buy or sell. **His number is 666**.

Turning to history we find that there is someone who fulfills everything predicted to the minutest detail.

HISTORICAL FULFILLMENT:

The second beast has two horns like a lamb. It is quite clear the intent here is to suggest that the face or façade of the second face, or side, of the beast will appear like a lamb, or Christianity. This false church, even though it will speak lies for Satan the dragon, will present itself as the only true church. This is the ultimate cover – mimic the one you want to destroy. Have the feel, look, and sound of the real church and, as Scripture says, none of the power.

This side of the beast will do incredible feats of deception. There have been no other religions or movements that have claimed more signs and miracles to their endorsement than has the Roman Catholic Church. One sign in particular should be noted since the prophecy here speaks about it – called "making fire," it has been said to have occurred when images have come down and lighted their own candles. Let us not forget the crucifixes that have spoken, idols that sweat or have eyes that move, hands that move, images with mouths that open, the stigmata appearing on the hand or feet of the faithful and, of course, Mary has appeared to many. This is still claimed to be happening, even now in the 21st Century.

Catholic parishes (where Catholics living in the area are required to register and attend the church in that specific parish) are a direct result of a holdover from centuries of strict control by the Papacy. Pope Alexander III decreed, at the Third Lateran Council in 1178, that Catholics were not to trade with heretics. Pope Martin IV issued a decree preventing heretics from buying, selling, and owning property. If you did not bend your will to the popes and take the mark of the beast, you could not buy or sell just as prophecy predicted would come upon the true believers.

666 – The earliest solution to the meaning of the number was proposed by Irenaeus in the second century. He believed it to be the name LATEINOS [Greek for Latin]. Since the fourth kingdom was Rome, then the beast would be a Latin church in a Latin world. Dr. More reminds us, "They latinize everything: mass, prayers, hymns, litanies, canons, decretals, and bulls are conceived in Latin." In the Hebrew language, "Roman" happens to equal 666. The Holy Roman Catholic Church's calling card was definitely Latin and the Apostle John's prophecy has most certainly come true and clearly points to the Catholic Church; the Revived Rome. Again, we see that Scripture's warnings were absolutely fulfilled by the Holy Roman Catholic Church.

IT WAS DONE TO APPEAR AS A LAMB, OR TRUE CHURCH!

My former pastor, while in Europe ministering, scheduled some time out to do research. He returned with the following document that he shared with me. I have it in both the original as well as the English translation.

Declaration of the Roman Catholic Cardinals To Pope Giulio III Carried in 1550.

"Of all the advice we can give to your holiness we have left the most **necessary to the end.** [Most important] We must open our eyes well and use every effort available to us, and that is to allow the **reading of the Gospel to be made as little as possible**, [the Gospel, the truth is dangerous] especially in modern day language, [the common language other than Latin] in all those countries under our jurisdiction, to limit that part of the Gospel which is usually read during Mass, and to not allow any further reading of it. As long as the people are satisfied with such limitation [this is when someone else determines what you know] our interests will prosper, but as soon as the people want more, [the truth] our interests will fail. The Holy Bible is that book which more than any thing has made [them] rise up against us those tumults and storms whose causes were lost. In fact, if anyone should accurately examine and compare the teachings of the Bible with those made by our church [official Roman Catholic traditions and doctrines] **he will soon find a difference, and comprehend that our teachings are often different from the Bible and even contrary to it.** [They are opposite of truth] If the people [Catholics] realize this they will make no objections to challenge us until everything comes to light and we will become the subject of mockery and universal hatred, thus it is necessary to hide the Bible [truth, the Gospel, will set you free] from the sight of the people but with extreme precautions so not to cause rebellions."

God tells us that they would knowingly mimic the true church, and this was fulfilled exactly.

REVELATION 14:1-5
The Lamb and the 144,000

This subject of the 144,000 and the first fruits were covered and discussed in Chapter seven.

REVELATION 14:6-13
The Three Angels

"Then I saw another angel flying in midair, and he had the eternal gospel to proclaim to those who live on the earth - to every nation, tribe, language and people. He said in a loud voice, 'Fear God and give him glory, because the hour of his judgment has come. Worship him who made the heavens, the earth, the sea and the springs of water.' A second angel followed and said, 'Fallen! Fallen is Babylon the Great, which made all the nations drink the maddening wine of her adulteries.' A third angel followed them and said in a loud voice: 'If anyone worships the beast and his image and receives his mark on the forehead or on the hand, he, too, will drink of the wine of God's fury, which has been poured full strength into the cup of his wrath. He will be tormented with burning sulfur in the presence of the holy angels and of the Lamb. And the smoke of their torment rises forever and ever. There is no rest day or night for those who worship the beast and his image, or for anyone who receives the mark of his name.' This calls for patient endurance on the part of the saints who obey God's commandments and remain faithful to Jesus. Then I heard a voice from heaven say, 'Write: Blessed are the dead who die in the Lord from now on.' 'Yes,' says the Spirit, 'they will rest from their labor, for their deeds will follow them.'"

CLUES: Rev 14:6-13
An angel has the **eternal gospel to proclaim to all**. We previously discussed the printing and distribution of the Scriptures. What happens in history as a result of revealing and proclaiming the Truth?
Fallen is **Babylon.** Who is Babylon?
What happens to those who worship **the beast** and take his mark?
What happens to those who **die for Christ**?

The Final Trumpet

The events that followed the proclaiming of the eternal gospel are now history. They include the missionary era with the Great Awakening that swept Europe and North America due to many prominent men like the Wesley's, Whitefield, Edwards, Finney, etc. The hour had come for the impending destruction of Babylon (Holy Roman Catholic Church) who has made all nations drink of the wine of the wrath of her fornication. This combines two thoughts or metaphors. One, she has caused them to be seduced by the harlot church. The other, she had caused them to receive God's wrath. Babylon was the center of idolatry and rebellion against God. In like manner, Rome was the center of deception and idolatry. Those who serve the beast and receive his mark are going to be judged harshly. They will be tormented night and day and will receive no rest. This is why it is critical that those caught in the deception are given the truth so that they can decide their fate with all the facts. There are many who have been, and continue to be, deceived by Satan in ways that are too numerous to count. Remember, God tells us Satan's time is short and he knows it. His goal is to take as many with him as he is able.

What happens to those who die for Christ? They are regarded as blessed and their works follow them. When one dies, all wealth, lands, honors, position, and titles die and remain here. Yet, God declares what is done in Christ is held in account for you. God does what the ancient pharaohs only hoped could be true. They built their elaborate chambers and filled them with what they thought would be needed in the after life. Our God tells us that He has prepared a mansion for us. He will have a feast awaiting us. All that we desire has been bought and paid for by Christ. All that is His is ours. We have been made joint heirs with Christ. He will provide us with a new earth, a new heaven, and new bodies. What more could one desire?

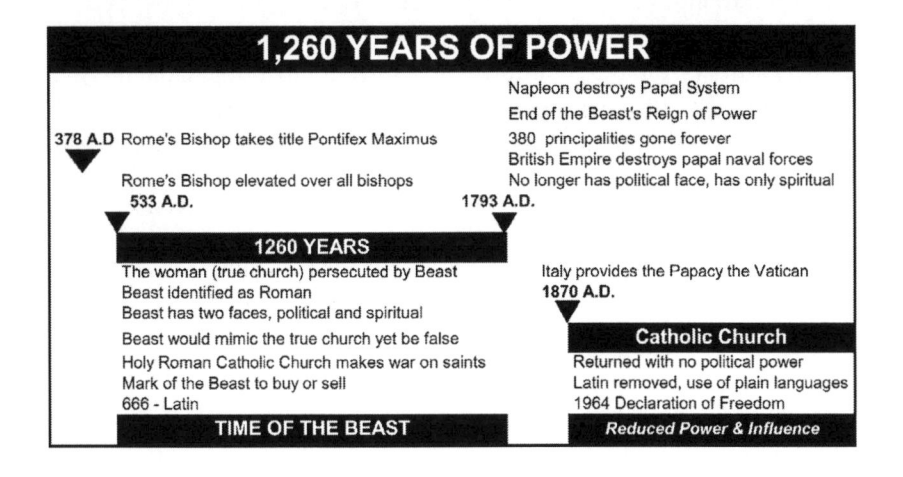

1,260 YEARS OF POWER

	Napleon destroys Papal System
	End of the Beast's Reign of Power
378 A.D Rome's Bishop takes title Pontifex Maximus	380 principalities gone forever
▼	British Empire destroys papal naval forces
Rome's Bishop elevated over all bishops	No longer has political face, has only spiritual
533 A.D.	**1793 A.D.** ▼

1260 YEARS	
The woman (true church) persecuted by Beast	Italy provides the Papacy the Vatican
Beast identified as Roman	**1870 A.D.** ▼
Beast has two faces, political and spiritual	
Beast would mimic the true church yet be false	**Catholic Church**
Holy Roman Catholic Church makes war on saints	Returned with no political power
Mark of the Beast to buy or sell	Latin removed, use of plain languages
666 - Latin	1964 Declaration of Freedom
TIME OF THE BEAST	*Reduced Power & Influence*

REVELATION 14:14-20
The Harvest of the Earth

"I looked, and there before me was a white cloud, and seated on the cloud was one 'like a son of man' with a crown of gold on his head and a sharp sickle in his hand. Then another angel came out of the temple and called in a loud voice to him who was sitting on the cloud, 'Take your sickle and reap, because the time to reap has come, for the harvest of the earth is ripe.' So he who was seated on the cloud swung his sickle over the earth, and the earth was harvested. Another angel came out of the temple in heaven, and he too had a sharp sickle. Still another angel, who had charge of the fire, came from the altar and called in a loud voice to him who had the sharp sickle, Take your sharp sickle and gather the clusters of grapes from the earth's vine, because its grapes are ripe.' The angel swung his sickle on the earth, gathered its grapes and threw them into the great winepress of God's wrath. They were trampled in the winepress outside the city, and blood flowed out of the press, rising as high as the horses' bridles for a distance of 1,600 stadia."

This section speaks to both the believer and non-believer. One angel has a sickle in hand to harvest the wheat (true believers). This is a great reassurance for the believers that this great day will come. This is obviously given as encouragement for believers as they remain faithful under trial and persecution.

The second angel is to harvest the grapes (non believers) and bring them to the winepress of God's wrath. Here we have a picture of the wicked being judged and trampled.

The number 1,600 is thought to indicate the universality of the judgment. The Scriptures reveal to us that forty (40) is the number of judgment. 1,600, then being 40 x 40, represents the enormity and universal nature of this coming judgment. The detail that the blood will rise as high as a horse bridle may be added for effect. It does get one's attention.

REVELATION 15
Seven Angles With Seven Pkagues

"I saw in heaven another great and marvelous sign: seven angels with the seven last plagues—last, because with them God's wrath is completed. And I saw what looked like a sea of glass mixed with fire and, standing beside the sea, those who had been victorious over the beast and his image and over the number of his name. They held harps given them by God and sang the song of Moses the servant of God and the song of the Lamb: 'Great and marvelous are your deeds, Lord God Almighty. Just and true are your ways, King of the ages. Who will not fear you, O Lord, and bring glory to your name? For you alone are holy. All nations will come and worship before you, for your righteous acts have been revealed.' After this I looked and in heaven the temple, that is, the tabernacle of the Testimony, was opened. Out of the temple came the seven angels with the seven plagues. They were dressed in clean, shining linen and wore golden sashes around their chests. Then one of the four living creatures gave to the seven angels seven golden bowls filled with the wrath of God, who lives forever and ever. And the temple was filled with smoke from the glory of God and from his power, and no one could enter the temple until the seven plagues of the seven angels were completed."

The seven angels have the last seven plagues. The Beast (The Roman Catholic Church) is now to be defeated. The angels are each given a golden bowl of God's wrath to pour out. The seven plagues are contained within the seventh trumpet of Revelation 8:1, which extends to the end of history and the return of Christ. Even though the seven angels pour in rapid succession in this vision, in earth's time it covers over two centuries.

REVELATION 16
The Seven Bowls of God's Wrath

"Then I heard a loud voice from the temple saying to the seven angels, 'Go, pour out the seven bowls of God's wrath on the earth.'

The first angel went and poured out his bowl on the land, and ugly and painful sores broke out on the people who had the mark of the beast and worshiped his image.

The second angel poured out his bowl on the sea, and it turned into blood like that of a dead man, and every living thing in the sea died.

The third angel poured out his bowl on the rivers and springs of water, and they became blood. Then I heard the angel in charge of the waters say: 'You are just in these judgments you who are and who were, the Holy One, because you have so judged; for they have shed the blood of your saints and prophets, and you have given them blood to drink as they deserve.' And I heard the altar respond: 'Yes, Lord God Almighty, true and just are your judgments.'

The fourth angel poured out his bowl on the sun, and the sun was given power to scorch people with fire. They were seared by the intense heat and they cursed the name of God, who had control over these plagues, but they refused to repent and glorify him.

The fifth angel poured out his bowl on the throne of the beast, and his kingdom were plunged into darkness. Men gnawed their tongues in agony and cursed the God of heaven because of their pains and their sores, but they refused to repent of what they had done.

The sixth angel poured out his bowl on the great river Euphrates, and its water was dried up to prepare the way for the kings from the East. Then I saw three evil spirits that looked like frogs; they came out of the mouth of the dragon, out of the mouth of the beast and out of the mouth of the false prophet. They are spirits of demons performing miraculous signs, and they go out to the kings of the whole world, to gather them for the battle on the great day of God Almighty. 'Behold, I come like a thief! Blessed is he who stays awake and keeps his clothes with him, so that he may not go naked and be shamefully exposed.' Then they gathered the kings together to the place that in Hebrew is called Armageddon."

The seventh angel poured out his bowl into the air, and out of the temple came a loud voice from the throne, saying, 'It is done!' Then there came flashes of lightning, rumblings, peals of thunder and a severe earthquake. No earthquake like it has ever occurred since man has been on earth, so

The Final Trumpet

tremendous was the quake. The great city split into three parts, and the cities of the nations collapsed. God remembered Babylon the Great and gave her the cup filled with the wine of the fury of his wrath. Every island fled away and the mountains could not be found. From the sky huge hailstones of about a hundred pounds each fell upon men. And they cursed God on account of the plague of hail, because the plague was so terrible."

CLUES: Rev 16

What do the bowls represent? A series of calamities.

HISTORICAL FULFILLMENT: THE FIRST BOWL

The first bowl is poured on those who had the mark of the beast. This was understood to mean, "those who sustained the civil or secular power to which the Papacy gave life and strength, and from which it, in turn, received countenance and protection." (Barnes) Robert Flemming wrote two key books in the first decade of the 18th Century. They were The Apocalyptic Key and The Rise and Fall of the Papacy. Great Britain had broken away and was now ruled by William II, a Protestant king. William III deposed of James II, who tried to bring back the Roman Catholic Church as the state religion. In 1690, Flemming informed William III that the bowl of wrath would be poured out in 1793-94 on the Roman Catholic Church. Flemming knew history recorded in 533 A.D. that the bishop of Rome was elevated over all bishops with the Justinian decree. Counting forward using the day for year he saw the beginning of God's wrath in 1793-94.

The major event in Europe directly impacting the Papacy in the year 1793, was the French Revolution. The King of France had been a solid source of support, even being referred to as "the eldest son of the church" by the Pope. France entered the Age of Reason. Reason was the new god. Law was passed on November 24, 1793, banning religious exercise. This included banning the Bible. It was the first time in the annals of history that a great nation had thrown off ALL religious principles and openly defied the power of heaven. Voltaire, the leader of the Enlightenment, declared the Bible was false. What made the Bible appear false was the deception and misapplication by the Roman Catholic Church. As a result, France declared war on the

FULFILLMENT (cont.):

ruling hierarchy, plunging Europe into the bloodiest war recorded since the fall of Rome in 476 A.D. The power base of the Catholic church would never recover. The revolution was aimed at the power of the Papacy. In five years, two million people were slain, including 24,000 priests. Forty thousand churches were made into stables. This was in France alone. We see the foul and loathsome sore implying impurity, causing a reaction to occur. Moral corruption, atheism, and dissolution of society spread throughout those countries where the beast and his image were worshipped. This affected every Catholic nation in Europe.

THE SECOND BOWL

The second bowl is poured out. The first was against the land, this next bowl is on the sea. What happens after 1793 to the Naval power of the Roman countries that supported the Papacy? 1793 A.D. starts the deadliest contest for the mastery of the seas between Protestant England and Catholic Europe. By 1805, over 600 ships of the Line, their largest war ship at that time, had been lost. This does not include the thousands of other vessels destroyed. 1793, Lord Hood crushes the French at Toulon. 1794, Lord Howe defeated the French at Ushant. 1795, Lord Bridgeport defeats the French and Dutch fleets at Cape Good Hope. 1798, the Spanish and Dutch are defeated off Cape St. Vincent and Campertown. 1798, Lord Nelson's victory over the French at the Nile; in 1801, Lord Nelson's victory at Copenhagen; and in 1805, Lord's Nelson's annihilation of the French at Talfalgar are recorded.

FULFILLMENT (cont.): THE THIRD BOWL

The third bowl is poured out and it is predicted to impact the river and streams. The third trumpet was also against the rivers and springs. They were in the same regions of Europe that were impacted when Attila the Hun fulfilled prophecy by destroying the Roman armies until the rivers and springs became polluted with the blood.

We see that this is exactly where it would take place. Looking to history, we find that France was not content on keeping her revolutionary philosophy to herself. She decided to impose this on her neighbors. Beginning in 1793, France invaded Germany, Austria, Switzerland, and Northern Italy. These wars occurred on the Rhine, the Po, and the Danube, as well as the Alpine streams of Piedmont and Lombardy. During the whole papal Europe, there had never been any war in any of these regions. This is where the Lutherans, Moravians, Hussites, Albigenses, Waldenses, Vaudois, and Huguenots willingly laid down their lives for the true faith of Jesus Christ and in defiance to the Papacy. The prophecy does say it would be the area of Christian martyrs. This region is exactly where prophecy predicted, and history fulfilled, the pouring out of the third bowl on the Roman Catholic Church.

THE FOURTH BOWL

The fourth angel poured out his bowl. The sun is to scorch men with fire. The "sun" is generally a symbol of a great leader or ruler. Most reformers saw this sun as none other than Napoleon Bonaparte. From 1796 to 1815, Napoleon was engaged in continuous war without a moment's cessation. Historian Dr. Keith writes on page 190 of <u>The Signs of the Times</u>, "Napoleon performed the miracles of genius. His achievements still dazzle, while they amaze the world. Within a space of eight years he scorched every kingdom in Europe, from Naples to Berlin, and from Lisbon to Moscow. Ancient kingdoms withered before the intense blaze of his power...Kingdoms were unsparingly rift like garments...like the sun, there was nothing hid from his great heat." In 1815, the Congress at Vienna attempted to restore the old order but the 380 principalities of pre-Napoleonic Europe would never reassemble again under the popes. All had been lost!

FULFILLMENT (cont.): THE FIFTH BOWL

The fifth angel poured out his bowl on the throne of the beast and his kingdom became full of darkness. They did not repent. The beast is the Papacy and the throne is in Rome. This prophecy indicates that the Pope's time of power is over and ending. However, "they do not repent" supports the concept that they will not be totally destroyed. They will survive in a new state.

Looking to history, we see that Rome's populace revolted as it, too, was swept up by the age of reason. December 27, 1797, Berthier, the commander of the French troops, received orders from the Directory to enter Italy and take Rome. The French exceeded the Goths and Vandels in their pillaging of Rome's treasures.

In 1798, Pope Pius VI was removed. The pope later died in exile at age 82. The historian Barnes writes, "In the year 1848, the pope was actually driven away to Gaeta, and… at this present time he is restored, though evidently with diminished power." Italian troops conquered Rome in 1870, and incorporated it back into the Kingdom of Italy.

Does the Papacy repent? No, the papacy responds with blasphemous declarations. In 1854, they issued the doctrine of the Immaculate Conception of Mary. They waited a long time to find this in Scripture. Oh, it is not there. Mary clearly acknowledged her need of a Savior for she proclaimed. "My soul doth magnify the Lord, and my spirit hath rejoiced in God my Savior" (Luke 1:46,47). Mary knew that she was human and that she needed a Savior. Jesus was the Son of God and the Son of Man. He left heaven, took human form and felt temptation, pain, etc., just like we do. Mary needed to be human if Jesus was to be the Son of Man as Scripture clearly says. One more example and we will move on. In 1870, the pope declares his infallibility when speaking ex cathedra… "The Roman pontiff, when he speaks ex cathedra…is, by reason of the Divine assistance promised to him in blessed Peter, possessed of infallibility… and consequently such definitions of the Roman Pontiff are irreformable." The quote is from the Catholic Encyclopedia. Vol. 7, p. 796, quoted by Caringola. This proclamation goes counter to all Scripture and exposes the pope as one who is not divine. If the pope was divine, then He would not blunder and say he has qualities that only God has demonstrated.

FULFILLMENT (cont.): THE SIXTH BOWL

The sixth angel poured out his bowl on the great river Euphrates and it dried up. This would make way for the rise of the kings, or power, from the east. Three unclean spirits would be at work during the 20th Century. Earlier described related to the sixth trumpet, the Turks were identified as being held back by the Euphrates. The Turkish Empire eventually crossed, conquered the Byzantine Empire, and became the Ottoman Empire. This empire now has the Sixth Bowl poured out upon it, which tells us that this empire will disappear or collapse.

History reveals that the once great Turkish Empire was defeated by the British Empire. In October 1917, General Edmund Allenby launched an attack on Turkish forces controlling Palestine and thus Jerusalem. The Turkish Empire ceased to exist as a result of World War I.

The collapse of the Turkish Empire is tied to another event in the same sentence. The kings of the east rise when the Turkish Empire is gone. The next deadly ideology and anti-Christian philosophy rose October 1917, in Russia's October Revolution. The next sentence of prophecy speaks of three unclean spirits from the dragon, or Satan, himself.

"Then I saw three evil spirits that looked like frogs; they came out of the mouth of the dragon, out of the mouth of the beast and out of the mouth of the false prophet."

The beast is the Papacy. The identity of the false prophet is clear. The fifth trumpet identified Islam rising up as a religion that is anti-Christian. Remember, conversion by the sword. Mohammad reduces Jesus Christ from Messiah to prophet. He elevates himself as the last and greatest prophet. The false prophet clearly identifies for us the second major force of the 20th Century against God's true church. The third is told to us in the sentence prior. It is Communism (Ottoman Empire falls and the power of the East rises; both occurred in October 1917). Looking back over the last century, the Papacy continues their non-repentance; Islamic countries do not allow Christianity and Communism is clearly anti-God. The Apostle John wrote this in the first century and yet named the three major anti-Christian forces at work in the world at the end of the 20th Century.

FULFILLMENT (cont.): THE SIXTH BOWL

The sixth bowl contains **Armageddon.** It is after the fall of the Turkish Empire and prior to the pouring of the seventh bowl.

"They are spirits of demons performing miraculous signs, and they go out to the kings of the whole world, to gather them for the battle on the great day of God Almighty. 'Behold, I come like a thief! Blessed is he who stays awake and keeps his clothes with him, so that he may not go naked and be shamefully exposed.' **Then they gathered the kings together to the place that in Hebrew is called Armageddon.**"

There are three false powers that oppose true Christianity in the 20th Century. They will assemble the kings of this earth in all their power for a great day (a day in the Lord is not limited to one day of our time) of battle. This battle will belong to the Lord. He will come and expose their bankrupt philosophies. He will make them naked, suggesting that God's truth will expose Communism, Islam, Catholicism, Humanism, and the myriad of other philosophies of men, for the lies that they are. Interesting that the Apostle John states that the place in Hebrew is called Armageddon. We need to understand from the Hebrew mindset what John is saying. Armageddon is literally spelled Har-Magedon, meaning Mount Megiddo. There is a plain of Megiddo, but no mount or mountain of Megiddo. This is obviously meant to be taken symbolically, since no literal place exists. What does the Apostle John want us to see? First, we need to think like someone in his time. The rule is always to consider to whom the writer is writing. This was written to the church. The purpose is to give the church hope and the confidence that God is in control of all the events in history. All history is moving according to His divine plan. Megiddo is listed among the conquests of Joshua (Josh 12:21). It is where Deborah defeated the kings of Canaan (Judges 5:19). It is where the evil grandson of King Ahab of Israel died (2 Kings 9:29). It is the place where Judah's King Josiah and the Egyptian Pharaoh Neco met defeat. Therefore, Armageddon is meant to be the symbolic place where evil is defeated or overcome by the truth of Christ, His Word, and His Church. This leads us to the seventh and final bowl.

FULLFILLMENT (cont.): THE SEVENTH BOWL

The seventh bowl contains the following:
"The seventh angel poured out his bowl into the air, and out of the temple came a loud voice from the throne, saying, 'It is done!' Then there came flashes of lightning, rumblings, peals of thunder and a **severe earthquake**. No earthquake like it has ever occurred since man has been on earth, so tremendous was the quake. The **great city split into three parts**, and the cities of the nations collapsed. God remembered Babylon the Great and gave her the cup filled with the wine of the fury of his wrath. Every island fled away and the mountains could not be found. From the sky huge hailstones of about a hundred pounds each fell upon men. And they cursed God on account of the plague of hail, because the plague was so terrible."

If you remember, a great earthquake with the sun, moon, stars, mountains, and islands being impacted and changed represents the sixth seal. It affected kings, princes, generals, rich, mighty, slave, and every free man. The one who brings the change sits on the throne and is the Lamb, an obvious reference to Christ, "The Lamb of God." For the day of wrath has come on those in religious power. The pagans' religions in this next period appear to be impacted. The sun and moon represent authority. The **stars** falling from the sky indicate the apostate beliefs are going to fall. The **moon** going dark indicates from Scripture that light will shine through darkness; in this case probably the Church overcomes. **Mountains** always represented a symbol of strength, majesty, and stability, whether talking about kingdoms, man, or God. Since the verses state they are "**removed from its place**," they would suggest that the earth's stability is going to be turned upside down by the Lamb.

1- Angel poured his bowl into the air – this tells us that we are looking for is something that happens in the atmosphere surrounding the earth.
2- A severe earthquake – no earthquake has ever been like it. This event will change the relationship of nations dramatically. Things will turn upside down.

FULFILLMENT (cont.):
CLUES:

3- It will affect three entities – the Great City is obviously symbolic. However, it will divide or represent three powers that dominate history during the 20th & 21st Centuries.

4- The hailstones are symbolic.

There is a coming judgment from God on Babylon the Great. Babylon the Great is reference to **all false religions** that have their roots in the original religion of Babylon that today, in the 21st Century, has so many different faces that one cannot believe they are all related to Babylon. There are a couple of things that are obvious here. The false religions of this world are going to be judged and found wanting by God. Men who believe in them will curse God as He brings His divine judgment on their false religions. They will be exposed as false.

The Sixth Bowl was in the year 1917. It was the predicted collapse of the Ottoman (Turks) Empire and the appearing of an anti-Christian, anti-God power to the East we now know as Communism.

The Seventh Bowl has either happened or is still in the future. We need to look over history for an event that would, in essence, redefine how the nations of this world relate to each other. The great city [earth] does not exist and is a symbol pointing to the whole world. This earthquake is so severe that the whole earth and every nation is affected. It will impact how nations relate to each other. The three major political entities are indicated. History clearly shows there are "Free" nations, Communist nations, and Islamic nations that are in an epic struggle against each other. Scripture says the cities of the nations collapse. What makes things collapse? Fear of sudden death, possibility of an all-encompassing war, another devastating terrorist attack, global disease outbreaks, etc. Governments have always been seen as the protector of their people. This prophecy seems to suggest that governments will no longer be able to guarantee this protection. The threat of the hailstones from the sky has become a plague to mankind. It would hang over their heads and cause them to live in constant fear of this. Mankind would curse the day the seventh angel poured this into the air. Whatever it is, the seventh

FULFILLMENT (cont.):

bowl neutralizes the strength of the powerful countries to where all are equal. This is the great earthquake that could destabilize all political options and relations for the 20th and 21st Centuries.

We must review the last century beginning with 1917 for one event that could cause this kind of political change.

On July 16, 1945, the history of the world forever changed. It had such an impact on our lives that it single-handedly altered how man views his security.

We lost it that day. That day small nations, terrorist groups, and the powerful nations all became equal. In a memo dated July 22, 1943, Winston Churchill – even before it was proven – feared that this was "…something that might be used for international blackmail." July 16, 1945, is the day when the seventh angel poured his bowl into the air and changed all political rules. The first atomic bomb known as "Gadget" exploded with a force of 20,000 tons of TNT.

Robert Oppenheimer, director of the Manhattan Project said this: "It is a profound and necessary truth that the deep things in science are not found because they are useful; they are found because it was possible to find them." We had opened Pandora's box. It has changed completely the price of war and we cannot go back and undo it. It is the curse from the sky. I remember as a child running home during the sounding of the sirens. I remember watching movies or reading books that were about the end of life and nuclear holocaust. Every weapon man has invented, he eventually uses, and so we did!

On August 6, an atomic bomb named "Little Boy" exploded above the city of Hiroshima. 66,000 people died instantly and 69,000 people were injured. By the end of that year, the death toll was approximately 140,000. This was only an 18,000 ton TNT explosion.

On August 9, 1945, an atomic bomb named "Fat Man" was dropped on the city of Nagasaki. 39,000 people died and another 25,000 people were injured that day. The only reason more did not die was that it was dropped over one mile off-target.

General Omar N. Bradley, Chief of Staff, United States Army, realizing what man had done, said this in 1948: "We have too many men of science, too few men of God. We grasped the mystery of the atom and rejected the Sermon on the Mount…The world has achieved brilliance without wisdom, power without conscience. Ours is a world of nuclear giants and ethical infants. We know more about war than we know about peace, more about killing than we know about living."

We now wait for only one event - the seventh (final) trumpet!

REVELATION 17
The Woman on the Beast

"One of the seven angels who had the seven bowls came and said to me, 'Come, I will show you the punishment of the great prostitute, who sits on many waters. With her the kings of the earth committed adultery and the inhabitants of the earth were intoxicated with the wine of her adulteries.' Then the angel carried me away in the Spirit into a desert. There I saw a woman sitting on a scarlet beast that was covered with blasphemous names and had seven heads and ten horns. The woman was dressed in purple and scarlet, and was glittering with gold, precious stones and pearls. She held a golden cup in her hand, filled with abominable things and the filth of her adulteries. This title was written on her forehead: MYSTERY BABYLON THE GREAT THE MOTHER OF PROSTITUTES AND OF THE ABOMINATIONS OF THE EARTH. I saw that the woman was drunk with the blood of the saints, the blood of those who bore testimony to Jesus. When I saw her, I was greatly astonished. Then the angel said to me: 'Why are you astonished? I will explain to you the mystery of the woman and of the beast she rides, which has the seven heads and ten horns. The beast, which you saw, once was, now is not, and will come up out of the Abyss and go to his destruction. The inhabitants of the earth whose names have not been written in the book of life from the creation of the world will be astonished when they see the beast, because he once was, now is not, and yet will come. This calls for a mind with wisdom. The seven heads are seven hills on which the woman sits. They are also seven kings. Five have fallen, one is, the other has not yet come; but when he does come, he must remain for a little while. The beast who once was, and now is not, is an eighth king. He belongs to the seven and is going to his destruction. The ten horns you saw are ten kings who have not yet received a kingdom, but who for one hour will receive authority as kings along with the beast. They have one purpose and will give their power and authority to the beast. They will make war against the Lamb, but the Lamb will overcome them because he is Lord of lords and King of kings—and with him will be his called, chosen and faithful followers.' Then the angel said to me, 'The waters you saw, where the prostitute sits, are peoples, multitudes, nations and languages. The beast and the ten horns you saw will hate the prostitute.

They will bring her to ruin and leave her naked; they will eat her flesh and burn her with fire. For God has put it into their hearts to accomplish his purpose by agreeing to give the beast their power to rule, until God's words

The Final Trumpet

are fulfilled. The woman you saw is the great city that rules over the kings of the earth.'"

> ## CLUES: Rev 17
>
> **Who is the woman sitting on a scarlet beast that was covered with blasphemous names and had seven heads and ten horns?** Two clues are identified. First, seven hills; second ten horns, which this section clarifies by stating they are ten kings or kingdoms.
> **Who is the "MYSTERY BABYLON THE GREAT THE MOTHER OF PROSTITUTES AND OF THE ABOMINATIONS OF THE EARTH?"** This states that whomever we decide this is, there is a direct link to the Babylonian false religion.
> **This woman was drunk with the blood of the saints.** This points us to someone who will kill the true saints of God.
> **They see the beast, because he once was, now is not, and yet will come.** We need to use this to see how history actually fulfills Scripture. Someone who was against the true Church (Rome up to 313 A.D.); then, for a period of time will not be against the true Church. (Rome after Christianity is elevated as the Empire's official religion) Finally, it will once again be against the true Church. (The Holy Roman Church)
> **The seven heads are seven hills on which the woman sits. They are also seven kings. Five have fallen, one is, the other has not yet come; but when he does come, he must remain for a little while. The beast who once was, and now is not, is an eighth king.** The seven hills are a reference to Rome. The seven kings are another clue. Five are past, the sixth is the present, the seventh comes later, and the eighth is the beast.
> **The ten horns are ten kings who have not yet received a kingdom.** Here it is telling us exactly who the ten horns [kingdoms] are and how short their rule will be.
> Once again, we will turn to history. We will look for history and Revelation to fit together without any effort other than to find the match.

HISTORICAL FULFILLMENT:

Why do you marvel? The angel is here to set the record absolutely straight. He will tell us the information to ensure that we know exactly who the beast is. The seven heads or hills again identify the beast as Rome. The ten horns, or kingdoms, are once again identified as formerly noted. Previously, we have shown that the beast killed the saints of the true and living God. However, the next item is new and is given to further prepare and identify the course of events that are going to unfold.

"Five have fallen, one is, the other has not yet come; but when he does come, he must remain for a little while. The beast who once was, and now is not, is an eighth king." Turning to history H. Gratten Guinness on page 168 of his great work <u>The Approaching End of the Age</u> identified these distinct forms of Roman power: "The great Roman power did actually exist under seven distinct… forms of government, enumerated by Livy, Tacitus, and historians in general, as such. Rome was ruled by KINGS, CONSULS, DICTATORS, DECEMVIRS, MILITARY TRIBUNES, MILTARY EMPERORS [Caesars], AND DESPOTIC EMPERORS, [emphasis]."

Five have fallen or are past. The sixth is in power at the Apostle John's time. This was an historical fact. The next was the succession of Emperors that would follow the Caesars. The eighth would be Roman and it rose from the ashes after Rome fell in 476 A.D. The Papacy has always declared it is Roman. The pope, to this very century still claims the title: Pontifex Maximus, which was held by all Roman emperors. There is no mystery here, only revelation that points to the Roman Catholic Church as the beast. History has recorded for all to see that the Papacy in fact waged wars against the true saints of God for 1,260 years. History reveals that the Papacy rose up in 533 A.D, lasted 1,260 years with the end coming by Napoleon in 1793-94, just as revealed in Scripture.

REVELATION 18
The Fall of Babylon

"After this I saw another angel coming down from heaven. He had great authority, and the earth was illuminated by his splendor. With a mighty voice he shouted: 'Fallen! Fallen is Babylon the Great! She has become a home for demons and a haunt for every evil spirit, a haunt for every unclean and detestable bird. For all the nations have drunk the maddening wine of her adulteries. The kings of the earth committed adultery with her, and the merchants of the earth grew rich from her excessive luxuries.' Then I heard another voice from heaven say: "Come out of her, my people, so that you will not share in her sins, so that you will not receive any of her plagues; for her sins are piled up to heaven, and God has remembered her crimes. Give back to her as she has given; pay her back double for what she has done. Mix her a double portion from her own cup. Give her as much torture and grief as the glory and luxury she gave herself. In her heart she boasts, 'I sit as queen; I am not a widow, and I will never mourn.' Therefore in one day her plagues will overtake her: death, mourning and famine. She will be consumed by fire, for mighty is the Lord God who judges her. When the kings of the earth who committed adultery with her and shared her luxury see the smoke of her burning, they will weep and mourn over her. Terrified at her torment, they will stand far off and cry: 'Woe! Woe, O great city, O Babylon, city of power! In one hour your doom has come!' The merchants of the earth will weep and mourn over her because no one buys their cargoes any more - cargoes of gold, silver, precious stones and pearls; fine linen, purple, silk and scarlet cloth; every sort of citron wood, and articles of every kind made of ivory, costly wood, bronze, iron and marble; cargoes of cinnamon and spice, of incense, myrrh and frankincense, of wine and olive oil, of fine flour and wheat; cattle and sheep; horses and carriages; and bodies and souls of men. They will say, 'The fruit you longed for is gone from you. All your riches and splendor have vanished, never to be recovered.' The merchants who sold these things and gained their wealth from her will stand far off, terrified at her torment.

They will weep and mourn and cry out. 'Woe! Woe, O great city, dressed in fine linen, purple and scarlet, and glittering with gold, precious stones and pearls! In one hour such great wealth has been brought to ruin!' Every sea captain, and all who travel by ship, the sailors, and all who earn their living from the sea, will stand far off. When they see the smoke of her burning, they will exclaim, 'Was there ever a city like this great city?' They will throw dust on their heads, and with weeping and mourning cry out: 'Woe! Woe, O great city, where all who had ships on the sea became rich through her wealth! In one hour she has been brought to ruin! Rejoice over her, O heaven! Rejoice, saints and apostles and prophets! God has judged her for the way she treated you.' Then a mighty angel picked up a boulder the size of a large millstone and threw it into the sea, and said: 'With such violence the great city of Babylon will be thrown down, never to be found again. The music of harpists and musicians, flute players and trumpeters, will never be heard in you again. No workman of any trade will ever be found in you again. The sound of a millstone will never be heard in you again. The light of a lamp will never shine in you again. The voice of bridegroom and bride will never be heard in you again. Your merchants were the world's great men. By your magic spell all the nations were led astray. In her was found the blood of prophets and of the saints, and of all who have been killed on the earth.'"

This was the future to the Apostle John. However, there are some very important messages for those who lived during the height of the Holy Roman Catholic Church's power and tyranny. First, the Holy Roman Catholic Church is identified as Babylon. Babylon is thrown down and it is implied here that a reduction of power is coming upon the Holy Roman Catholic Church. Second, God is going to pay her back with a double portion (twice as much as she did to the saints of God). Third, God tells those in the Catholic Church to come out. This is a direct command to rebuke the concept of ecumenism (one all encompassing universal church lacking real Biblical truth). The Roman Catholic Church continues to show signs of decline. Frequently, we hear news of Catholic schools closing or consolidating due to lack of student enrollment. There are other reported scandals concerning the many cover-ups of sexual abuse. The Roman Catholic Church's wealth is being literally eaten away by the lawyers and the many out-of-court settlements. God is still waiting for the Pope and his hierarchy to repent.

REVELATION 19:1-10
The Wedding of the Lamb

"After this I heard what sounded like the roar of a great multitude in heaven shouting: 'Hallelujah! Salvation and glory and power belong to our God, for true and just are his judgments. He has condemned the great prostitute who corrupted the earth by her adulteries. He has avenged on her the blood of his servants.' And again they shouted: 'Hallelujah! The smoke from her goes up for ever and ever.' The twenty-four elders and the four living creatures fell down and worshiped God, who was seated on the throne. And they cried: 'Amen, Hallelujah!' Then a voice came from the throne, saying: 'Praise our God, all you his servants, you who fear him, both small and great!' Then I heard what sounded like a great multitude, like the roar of rushing waters and like loud peals of thunder, shouting: 'Hallelujah! For our Lord God Almighty reigns. Let us rejoice and be glad and give him glory! For the wedding of the Lamb has come, and his bride has made herself ready. Fine linen, bright and clean, was given her to wear.' Then the angel said to me, 'Write: Blessed are those who are invited to the wedding supper of the Lamb!' And he added, 'These are the true words of God.' At this I fell at his feet to worship him. But he said to me, 'Do not do it! I am a fellow servant with you and with your brothers who hold to the testimony of Jesus. Worship God! For the testimony of Jesus is the spirit of prophecy.'"

If you are unfamiliar with some of the terminology, I will give you a quick background and review. Remember who the great multitude was? They were the saints who came through the great tribulation that started at the Day of Pentecost and ended at the Second Coming of Christ. It is the multitude that no man can count. The saints of God are assembled around the throne and are seen in praise of the Savior; the Lamb of God. The wedding of the Lamb (Christ) is an event promised in the New Testament (Matthew 22:1-4, parable of the marriage feast). The Bride of Christ is the true Church, made up of the believers who have accepted Jesus Christ as their Lord and Savior. The beginning of this chapter is simply to be read by believers and enjoyed. It speaks of coming events when we will be in the presence of the Divine and at the wedding feast that has been prepared for us.

REVELATION 19:11-16
KING OF KINGS

"I saw heaven standing open and there before me was a white horse, whose rider is called Faithful and True. With justice he judges and makes war. His eyes are like blazing fire, and on his head are many crowns. He has a name written on him that no one knows but he himself. He is dressed in a robe dipped in blood, and his name is the Word of God. The armies of heaven were following him, riding on white horses and dressed in fine linen, white and clean. Out of his mouth comes a sharp sword with which to strike down the nations. He will rule them with an iron scepter. He treads the winepress of the fury of the wrath of God Almighty. On his robe and on his thigh he has this name written: KING OF KINGS AND LORD OF LORDS. And I saw an angel standing in the sun, who cried in a loud voice to all the birds flying in midair, 'Come, gather together for the great supper of God, so that you may eat the flesh of kings, generals, and mighty men, of horses and their riders, and the flesh of all people, free and slave, small and great.' Then I saw the beast and the kings of the earth and their armies gathered together to make war against the rider on the horse and his army. But the beast was captured, and with him the false prophet who had performed the miraculous signs on his behalf. With these signs he had deluded those who had received the mark of the beast and worshiped his image. The two of them were thrown alive into the fiery lake of burning sulfur. The rest of them were killed with the sword that came out of the mouth of the rider on the horse, and all the birds gorged themselves on their flesh."

Here is the rest of the chapter. It is revealing the coming future events of glorious victory. True and faithful, with his armies dressed in white (robes of righteousness given to them by Christ) is able to deliver the winepress of God's fury. His name is **KING OF KINGS AND LORD OF LORDS**. The beast and the kings of this world who are under the direction and power of the dragon (Satan) gather together to make war. Jesus Christ, the Lamb of God who died on the cross for us, has appeared in his other role as the Lion of Judah. Jesus has overcome the beast (Papacy), the false prophet (Islam), and all those who have taken the mark of the beast. Their fate is sealed. Two were thrown into the Lake of Fire. The rest of the deceived will be condemned by His sword (the Word of God). Remember, warnings are given so we can act!

REVELATION 20:1-6
Two Expansions & Satan's Demise

"And I saw an angel coming down out of heaven, having the key to the Abyss and holding in his hand a great chain. He seized the dragon, that ancient serpent, who is the devil, or Satan, and **bound him [1]** for a thousand years. He threw him into the Abyss, and locked and sealed it over him, to keep him from deceiving the nations anymore until **the thousand years** were ended. After that, he [Satan] must be **set free for** a short time **[2]**. I saw thrones on which were seated those who had been given authority to judge. And I saw the souls of those who had been beheaded because of their testimony for Jesus and because of the word of God. They had not worshiped the beast or his image and had not received his mark on their foreheads or their hands. They came to life and reigned with Christ a thousand years. (The rest of the dead did not come to life until the thousand years were ended.) This is the first resurrection. Blessed and holy are those who have part in the first resurrection. The second death has no power over them, but they will be priests of God and of Christ and will reign with him for a thousand years. When the thousand years are over, **Satan will be released** from his prison **[3 & 4]** and will go out to deceive the nations in the four corners of the earth - Gog and Magog - to gather them for battle. In number they are like the sand on the seashore. They marched across the breadth of the earth and surrounded the camp of God's people, the city he loves. But fire came down from heaven and devoured them. And the devil, who deceived them, was thrown into the lake of burning sulfur, where the beast and the false prophet had been thrown. **[5]** They will be tormented day and night forever and ever. Then I saw a great white throne and him who was seated on it. Earth and sky fled from his presence, and there was no place for them. And I saw the dead, great and small, standing before the throne, and books were opened. Another book was opened, which is the book of life. The dead were judged according to what they had done as recorded in the books. The sea gave up the dead that were in it, and death and Hades gave up the dead that were in them, and each person was judged according to what he had done. Then death and Hades were thrown into the lake of fire. The lake of fire is the second death. If anyone's name was not found written in the book of life, he was thrown into the lake of fire."

[See Page 114]

What is this chapter telling us that we should be able to simply pull from history and the Holy Scriptures? It begins with the dragon. Satan is seized and bound for a period of time. Satan is thrown into the Abyss so as to reduce his influence and power over the nations of the world for a period of time. Satan is released, but for a short time. What is the result of Satan being released? The saints of God were beheaded because they would not worship the beast (Papacy) or receive his mark. This helps build the sequence. Satan's pagan nations had their way and paganism descended from the Babylon Mystery Religion as the religion of men. Do you remember what happens? Christ comes and is crucified and the Kingdom of God is established. The Holy Spirit comes and the Church is born. Based on this chapter, Satan is bound for a period of time. What happened to the Church in history? The Christian Church turns the world upside down and becomes the official religion of the Roman Empire in 326 A.D. History records, as we have already shown, that this event is followed by the period known as "The Rise of Christianity" and the Gospel is taken to the farthest reaches of the known world. Here in this chapter it states that Satan will be released for a short period of time. The next verses tell us exactly what Satan does. He helps empower the beast (Holy Roman Catholic Church) to assault the true saints of God for 1,260 years. They are part of the FIRST RESURRECTION. The Apostle John is being given a look at those who have died for their faith. They are well and are said to be BLESSED. We are told that those who are part of the **FIRST RESURRECTION** will not have to worry about the SECOND DEATH. They will reign with Christ for an unlimited period of time (the Bible says forever). The first resurrection is obtained when a person who is dead in sin accepts Jesus Christ as Lord and Savior. They that do this will not have to worry about the second death.

The thousand years here is symbolic. In Bible usage, one thousand is a round, indefinite number. Psalm 50:10 states, "Every beast of the forest is mine and the cattle on a thousand hills." Does it mean a thousand or is it symbolic? Deut 7:9, "God keeps his covenant and mercy to a thousand generations." Is God's mercy limited to a thousand generations? Of course not. He tells us his mercy endures forever. The one thousand here is symbolic. One final example, "He commanded His word to a thousand generations." Again, His Word is eternal and not limited to a period of time. The one thousand is symbolic of a period of indefinite time.

Satan is bound again and is in prison. This appears to be some time after the period of the beast, indicating that Satan was held in check again. The last time that Satan was held in check, Christianity overthrew paganism. If Satan was in prison and unable to help the beast, what would we expect to see history reveal about the Church? Incredible growth. History has such a period called the Reformation, followed by the three Great Awakenings, and worldwide missionary movements. Satan is released only to begin another attempt at a great deception (this appears to have begun in the 19th Century and continues into the 21st Century). He will deceive the nations from the four corners. Their numbers are like the sands on the seashore (today we are at six billion and growing). They will surround the camp of God's people. It appears that they will seem to have the upper hand. But wait! Fire comes down from heaven and devours them. This is the sudden and unexpected return of Jesus Christ at the sounding of the seventh and final trumpet Why? The next verse tells us that **Satan is thrown into the lake of burning sulfur with the beast and false prophet.** The key as to why this is at the second coming of Christ is the answer to the next question. They are tormented for how long? **FOREVER AND EVER!**

Once Christ has returned, the judgment follows. The Dead are judged first. Those who are not saved by Jesus Christ and have had the first resurrection in the spirit (re-born), are destined to stand before the **GREAT WHITE THRONE.** This is something that should motivate every believer to share the truth with everyone they know. I remember almost losing my life a few times and the realization of what was nearly my fate. I ran into two high school friends. I started to share with them about Christ and they told me they were Christians. I asked them when they came to know Christ. They informed me that they were both Christians in high school. I asked them why they hadn't told me about the truth of Christ when we were in school together. I told them I had almost died and that, ultimately, my eternity had been at stake!

At the Great White Throne, the **Book of Life** is opened. The dead are judged according to what they have done. If anyone's name is not in the Book of Life, they are thrown in the lake of fire, which is the second death!

Remember, I am just the messenger here. God is the one who has created this universe. He is the One who has created the parameters. Even if you disagree with His revelation, He is God and we are not. It matters not what my opinion is, it only matters what I do in response to what GOD has revealed to man in His divine book, the Bible.

REVELATION 20

This review is to highlight the sequence by numbers 1-5. [See page 264]

Satan status per Rev 20	Impact to History
[1] Satan seized, and locked in abyss No deceiving for period of time Remember 1000 is symbolic. [The key is when Satan is not free the church overcomes.]	Pagan Religions are world-wide Jesus sets up Kingdom of God Church given Great Commission Church rises becomes Empire's Offical Religion, next period known as Rise of the Church approx. 330 A.D. to 500 A.D.
[2] Satan is let free to help Beast Given a short period of time Saints beheaded by Beast Those who do not take mark are part of First Resurrection Second death has no power History shows reformation	Early 6th century Satan released By 533 A.D Bishop of Rome elevated over other bishops History shows the Beast martyred millions of Christians. This period lasts till about 1400 coming
[3] Satan is in prison [Church grows] Because in next verse he is released to again deceive. However, the beast [Catholic Church] is crushed. The Pope is put into prison 1798 without Satan loose to aid the beast.	While Satan in prison the Reformation begins and by 1517 it is official. With Satan in prison the Beast is destroyed by 1815. Napoleon predicted to reduce Holy Rome Catholic Church's power base forever. Great Awakenings, Gospel taken worldwide by missionaries
[4] Satan released from prison and will deceive all the nations from the four corners. Since Gospel taken world-wide by English and American Missionaries (other countries followed) This is final deception till the end Gather nations for battle, they will be like the sand, numerous	Satan would start again early 1800's The Beast back in Rome 1870. Rise of Evolution Deception 1859. Rise of Higher Criticism 1800's Secret Rapture Theory 1830's Marxism then Communism Attack against true Christianity Rise of false religions and cults More unbelievers alive now then at any other time in history.
[5] Fire came down, Satan thrown with beast and false prophet into the lake of fire.	Jesus returns. Beast & False Prophet are thrown in lake of fire in chapter 19 Chapter 20. We are informed Satan will join them.

Again, History and Scripture follow the same sequence. Satan is now in his final deception. He will deceive many as it says. However, as he rallies the nations against God he shall be defeated by the Rider on the White Horse who is Jesus returned.

REVELATION 21
The New Jerusalem

"Then I saw a new heaven and a new earth, for the first heaven and the first earth had passed away, and there was no longer any sea. I saw the Holy City, the new Jerusalem, coming down out of heaven from God, prepared as a bride beautifully dressed for her husband. And I heard a loud voice from the throne saying, 'Now the dwelling of God is with men, and he will live with them. They will be his people, and God himself will be with them and be their God. He will wipe every tear from their eyes. There will be no more death or mourning or crying or pain, for the old order of things has passed away.' He who was seated on the throne said, 'I am making everything new!' Then he said, 'Write this down, for these words are trustworthy and true.' He said to me: 'It is done. I am the Alpha and the Omega, the Beginning and the End. To him who is thirsty I will give to drink without cost from the spring of the water of life. He who overcomes will inherit all this, and I will be his God and he will be my son. But the cowardly, the unbelieving, the vile, the murderers, the sexually immoral, those who practice magic arts, the idolaters and all liars - their place will be in the fiery lake of burning sulfur. This is the second death.' One of the seven angels who had the seven bowls full of the seven last plagues came and said to me, 'Come, I will show you the bride, the wife of the Lamb.' And he carried me away in the Spirit to a mountain great and high, and showed me the Holy City, Jerusalem, coming down out of heaven from God.

It shone with the glory of God, and its brilliance was like that of a very precious jewel, like a jasper, clear as crystal. It had a great, high wall with twelve gates, and with twelve angels at the gates. On the gates were written the names of the twelve tribes of Israel. There were three gates on the east, three on the north, three on the south and three on the west. The wall of the city had twelve foundations, and on them were the names of the twelve apostles of the Lamb. The angel who talked with me had a measuring rod of gold to measure the city, its gates and its walls. The city was laid out like a square, as long as it was wide. He measured the city with the rod and found it to be 12,000 stadia in length, and as wide and high as it is long. He measured its wall and it was 144 cubits thick, by man's measurement, which the angel was using. The wall was made of jasper, and the city of pure gold, as pure as glass. The foundations of the city walls were decorated with every kind of precious stone. The first foundation was jasper, the second sapphire, the third chalcedony, the fourth emerald, the fifth sardonyx, the sixth carnelian, the seventh chrysolite, the eighth beryl, the ninth topaz, the tenth chrysoprase, the eleventh jacinth, and the twelfth amethyst. The twelve gates were twelve pearls, each gate made of a single pearl. The great street of the city was of pure gold, like transparent glass. I did not see a temple in the city, because the Lord God Almighty and the Lamb are its temple. The city does not need the sun or the moon to shine on it, for the glory of God gives it light, and the Lamb is its lamp. The nations will walk by its light, and the kings of the earth will bring their splendor into it. On no day will its gates ever be shut, for there will be no night there. The glory and honor of the nations will be brought into it. Nothing impure will ever enter it, nor will anyone who does what is shameful or deceitful, but only those whose names are written in the Lamb's book of life."

This is intended to give the believer a glimpse of what awaits those who overcome. It does not matter what your situation is in this world. If you are a believer, then this is going to uplift you and be a source of strength. There is a new heaven and earth coming – new, not repaired. God has prepared a city for us in which to dwell. Jesus told us he went away to prepare a mansion for each of us. The bride (the True Church) will be wed to Christ. We will dwell with God. God will wipe away our tears. What a place we will dwell in, a place of no death and no pain. Everything is made new. It has been accomplished and the battle has been won! Who has done such a thing? The Alpha and Omega! Who gets to enjoy this? He who overcomes! Remember all of the promises for those who overcome? We will be God's children. God will make us his sons and daughters, as well as joint heirs of all that Jesus Christ has. We will never have to face the second death.

The number twelve represents a place of completion and government. This is God's city with twelve gates and twelve angels at the gates. This represents the twelve tribes of Israel. It has three gates in each of the four directions. The walls have twelve foundations and on them the names of the twelve apostles of the Lamb. This is a city that is complete and in need of nothing. The measurements are in twelve or multiples of twelve. It is described as having streets of pure gold and walls made from precious jewels. This reveals the abundance that is found in God. This city will not need the sun or moon for light. It will be illuminated by the glory of God. The Lamb will be its lamp. We will live in the light and nothing impure will ever be. Imagine what this is going to be like. In 1516, English statesman Sir Thomas More penned a now famous description of an ideal commonwealth governed entirely by reason and free of crime, poverty, injustice, and other ills. The name More gave to his imaginary society of ideal perfection was UTOPIA, from the Greek meaning "NOWHERE." And well named it was, for there certainly was no such place anywhere in the world. This is the secret dream or

The Final Trumpet

wish of anyone who has seen the harsh reality of this world. God has prepared a place that our wildest dreams cannot fathom. It is for all those whose names are found in the Lamb's (Christ's) Book of Life.

At some point, whether it is now or later, you need to become totally selfish. You need to focus upon one thing – YOU! I used Deductive logic to do my analysis. It required overwhelming evidence to be considered as valid and worth acting upon. The question is: have you ever felt that there is something more, that this is not all there is? Listen to those inner feelings. God has so much more for each of us. It requires that you evaluate everything that you have ever learned. Is it possible that much of what a person has been taught is not true? Many of the things I was taught were a deception. I was told there was no God. I was told evolution was a fact. I was told the Bible is full of contradictions and fairy tales. I came to discover that the Bible is God's Revelation and full of prophecy. Prophecy, or the prediction of the future, shows that only God wrote the Bible. The Bible reveals the coming of the Messiah, Jesus Christ, who fulfilled over one hundred detailed prophecies and many when He was under the control of his enemies. The Greek Empire translated the Bible into Greek ensuring that prophecy was at least three hundred years old when fulfilled. Then it contains the rising and falling of empires, along with the timeline of events, from the beginning of the Church to the second coming of Christ. No one ever told me that God had revealed in Scripture a roadmap for history concerning his plans and showing His sovereign control of human affairs. To watch Revelation as a sequential series of events being fulfilled in history was incredible. The Apostle John, in the first century, provided detailed prophecy so that as it is fulfilled, it becomes clear to any who open their eyes and hearts. It is time for you to be selfish. What is the future of your soul in light of eternity? God asks you to decide.

REVELATION 22

"Then the angel showed me the river of the water of life, as clear as crystal, flowing from the throne of God and of the Lamb down the middle of the great street of the city. On each side of the river stood the tree of life, bearing twelve crops of fruit, yielding its fruit every month. And the leaves of the tree are for the healing of the nations. No longer will there be any curse. The throne of God and of the Lamb will be in the city, and his servants will serve him. They will see his face, and his name will be on their foreheads. There will be no more night. They will not need the light of a lamp or the light of the sun, for the Lord God will give them light. And they will reign forever and ever. The angel said to me, 'These words are trustworthy and true. The Lord, the God of the spirits of the prophets, sent his angel to show his servants the things that must soon take place. Behold, I am coming soon! Blessed is he who keeps the words of the prophecy in this book.' I, John, am the one who heard and saw these things. And when I had heard and seen them, I fell down to worship at the feet of the angel who had been showing them to me. But he said to me, 'Do not do it! I am a fellow servant with you and with your brothers the prophets and of all who keep the words of this book. Worship God!' Then he told me, 'Do not seal up the words of the prophecy of this book, because the time is near. Let him who does wrong continue to do wrong; let him who is vile continue to be vile; let him who does right continue to do right; and let him who is holy continue to be holy. Behold, I am coming soon! My reward is with me, and I will give to everyone according to what he has done. I am the Alpha and the Omega, the First and the Last, the Beginning and the End. Blessed are those who wash their robes, that they may have the right to the tree of life and may go through the gates into the city. Outside are the dogs, those who practice magic arts, the sexually immoral, the murderers, the idolaters and everyone who loves and practices falsehood. 'I, Jesus, have sent my angel to give you this testimony for the churches. I am the Root and the Offspring of David, and the bright Morning Star.' The Spirit and the bride say, 'Come!' And let him who hears say, "Come!" Whoever is thirsty, let him come; and whoever wishes, let him take the free gift of the water of life.

I warn everyone who hears the words of the prophecy of this book: If anyone adds anything to them, God will add to him the plagues described in this book. And if anyone takes words away from this book of prophecy, God will take away from him his share in the tree of life and in the holy city, which are described in this book. He who testifies to these things says, 'Yes,

The Final Trumpet

I am coming soon.' Amen. Come, Lord Jesus. The grace of the Lord Jesus be with God's people. Amen."

This is the final book of Revelation. This is a non-traditional and a unique reading of Revelation. Look at history and Revelation to find the matches in history starting at the beginning of the Church, where the Apostle John revealed we should start. I then concluded that God was in charge of history as revealed in His word, the Bible. Applying this to Revelation, it was then fantastic to see history and Revelation become one. I am in debt to the historians and Christians who recorded the past so diligently. It has made seeing God's fulfillment possible in the 21st Century. God is in control and He has already determined the outcome. God wants all to know the final outcome and the choices that are available to each.

Let's read the end of history and His revelation. May we listen and respond properly for these are truthfully the words of God Almighty!

Think of how beautiful it will be. God tells us there will be NO CURSE. The curse was time. Time is the true curse. It limits our ability to develop relationships. It limits the days that we have. God tells us in Psalm 90:10, "The length of our days is seventy years-or eighty, if we have the strength; yet their span is but trouble and sorrow, for they quickly pass, and we fly away." We get seventy years and, if we are strong, maybe eighty. Amazingly, the average age of death in America is between seventy and eighty. The truth is expounded for us again in James 4:14, "Why, you do not even know what will happen tomorrow. What is your life? You are a mist that appears for a little while and then vanishes." Anyone who has reached old age will tell you that life flew by just as God says. Think about this. Our first name is baby, our middle name is vapor (James 4:14) and our last name is corpse. Many think money is most important. They are wrong, it is time. Time is the great equalizer. Time is the most important…it is a delusion to think it is money, power or fame. Time was the curse. And it will be removed.

"These words are true and trustworthy. I am coming soon." Where are we in time? The seventh bowl appears to have happened in 1945. The final event is the intervention of Christ at the sounding of the seventh trumpet announcing His return. No man knows the time. However, every eye will see His return. God tells John not to seal up the Revelation. God tells us we will be blessed for reading this book. God has promised to give to everyone according to his deeds. This sounds like justice. Imagine standing before a judge whom you cannot deceive, who knows all. God makes his final offer, **"Whoever is thirsty, let him come; and whoever wishes, let him take the free gift of the water of life."**

Now comes an important warning: "anyone who adds, detracts, or alters the words of this book, God will add to him **PLAGUES** and removes his share in the **TREE OF LIFE.**"

It ends with "Yes, I am coming soon." Amen. Come, Lord Jesus. The grace of the Lord Jesus be with God's people. Amen."

THE FINAL WARNING

Why would God warn us that He would take away our share in the tree of life if we add or take away from His Word? This prophecy has been fulfilled over and over during the last two thousand years.

Many religious groups have the Bible as just one of some number of divine books. They have elevated something else either as equal or superior to God's word. Many religious movements have some later revelation from God that they believe in spite of the fact that it conflicts with the Bible.

Recently, during this generation, there is a move to change God the Father to an asexual being in the Bible by liberal theologians. Imagine you are standing in front of the Creator of all and have to explain why you disobeyed Him. God has made clear what the penalty is for tampering with the truth of His Word. Anything that is elevated as being equal to the Bible would qualify to receive this curse.

When tradition, or any other book or writing, is said to be equal to God's Holy and Perfect Word this would be considered making additions to the Bible. Those who go about teaching that anything outside of the Bible is God's Word need to consider the above warning from God. This practice comes at a steep price for those who do.

QUICK REVIEW

In Revelation since our last quick review, we covered Chapter 12 to the final book Chapter 22.

Chapter 12 - The Woman and Dragon are identified. The woman (Israel) is about to give birth to the Messiah. Satan, the red dragon, appears with seven heads pointed to Rome as his agent. Rome who is in power does try to kill baby Jesus and is unable. The woman becomes the church who is to be persecuted for 1,260 years. History clearly shows the Holy Roman Church as the one who made war against the true saints of God.

Chapter 13 - The two different faces of the beast are identified. The first face is the Beast out of the Sea is identified as Roman. Rome falls, but it rises again in a new form. We reviewed Daniel 7:15-28 since it provided multiple clues as to whom the beast was and what kinds of things he would do. The second face is the Beast out of the Earth. The warning is that the Holy Roman church will appear as a lamb, a Christian church and actually be the ultimate deception. The Holy Roman Catholic church became a "wolf" in Lamb's clothes. Again, History and Revelation matched completely.

Chapter 14 - Begins by revealing to us who the 144,000 are. They are the first fruits representing the first Jews to receive the gospel. Next come three angels with three announcements. The first was that the eternal gospel was to be proclaimed. The reformation was right on time and followed in the correct sequence. The second angel states Babylon is Fallen. Babylon's (Papacy) judgment is coming. The third angel warns not to worship the beast or take his mark. Whoever partakes of the mark of the beast will be judged harshly. Finally, the church is reminded that the day of judgment will come upon the beast and all who serve him.

Chapter 15 - John sees the Seven Angels with the final Seven Plagues. The Beast will be defeated. The seven plagues are poured out over the next two centuries. Each angel was given a bowl by one of the four living creatures.

Chapter 16 - The Sevens Bowls of God's Wrath are poured out. All seven bowls or seals have been revealed in history.

> **1st BOWL** - is poured on those who have the mark of the beast. We saw the Papacy was to have its power reduced. The Holy Roman Church started in 533 A.D. with the elevation of the Bishop of Rome above all other bishops. Adding 1,260 years brought us to the French Revolution (1793), the bloodiest war in Europe since the fall of Rome. The papacy would never recover its former power and glory.

2nd BOWL - is against the naval forces loyal to the popes. Protestant England crushes all the naval forces the papacy sent from its many loyal countries.

3rd BOWL - is against the nations of the rivers. Here we see the nations where the Christian Martyrs are avenged. France attacks Germany, Austria, Switzerland, and Northern Italy as prophesy stated.

4th BOWL - reveals a great leader that history clearly confirms as Napoleon. He did destroy the power base of the Holy Roman Church from 380 principalities to none. The pope ended up being thrown in jail.

5th BOWL - reveals the wrath of God is poured on the beast's throne. The pope does not repent, indicating the papacy will survive only in a new form with much less influence. History shows not until 1870 was the Catholic Church able to return to Rome. It returned back to the Vatican but has lost sway over nations and its control of the faithful continues to weaken as predicted.

6th BOWL - told us that the Ottoman Empire (Turks) was next to collapse. History records that event as October 1917. As we entered the 20th Century there were to be three major antichristian forces. The beast (Papacy), the false prophet (Islam) and the new king of the east (Communism). The Ottomans disappeared October 1917 and, in the same month, Communism appeared. This was predicted by the Apostle John in the first century.

7th- BOWL- was poured into the air. Political instability reigns. Terror from the sky hangs over our heads. July 16, 1945, began the nuclear age and its curse. The false religions of this world will be exposed.

Chapter 17- The angel of God with absolute certainty pointed us to the identity of the Woman on the Beast. First clue was the seven hills (Rome). Second clue was the ten kingdoms (Rome). Both pointed to the Papacy. Next, what she will do. The papacy will get drunk on the blood of the saints. This is followed with a clue that the Holy Roman Catholic Church is the eighth type of power to sit on Rome and calls her the beast. History records the Papacy was the eighth form of Roman power. This chapter takes many of the clues from the other chapters and puts them into one chapter and uses them all to insure the no one could miss the identity of the "Beast."

Chapter 18- tells us that Babylon the Great (Papacy) with all her wealth is doomed. Their riches will vanish and they will receive a double portion of God's wrath. Warnings are given so people can change sides by repenting.

The Final Trumpet

Chapter 19- moves its focus to the true church of God. God has avenged and has also prepared for the wedding of the Lamb to His bride the church. Next, Christ appears on a white horse and is called Faithful and True. The armies of heaven follow Him. His name is KING OF KINGS and LORD OF LORDS. The beast and false prophet are thrown into the LAKE OF FIRE. The rest are judged by the sword (Word of God).

Chapter 20- Many believe there is an actual 1000 year Millennium on earth after Christ's second coming. History and Revelation have been shown in their historical sequence and in complete alignment. Those who would not worship the beast or his image, or take the mark of the beast, will not suffer the second death. Satan's final demise is that he is thrown into the lake of fire with the beast and false prophet. Two additional groups of verses shed light on the reason why I leaned toward the thousand years being symbolic and not literal.

The first verse is found in Peter's second epistle. The order provides the sequence of events at the return of Christ. The time of the return of Christ is **UNKNOWN** and comes upon people like a thief. The present heavens, including the earth, disappear and are destroyed by fire. They are replaced with the new heaven and earth.

2 Peter 3:10-13, "But the day of the Lord will come like a thief. The **heavens will disappear** with a roar; the elements will be destroyed by fire, and the earth and everything in it will be laid bare. Since everything will be destroyed in this way, what kind of people ought you to be? You ought to live holy and godly lives as you look forward to the day of God and speed its coming. That day will bring about the destruction of the heavens by fire, and the elements will melt in the heat. But in keeping with his promise we are looking forward **to a new heaven and a new earth**, the home of righteousness."

These verses clearly state that the present earth is destroyed at the second coming of Christ. This would make it appear impossible to have a One Thousand Year Reign by Christ on the existing earth since it is nonexistent. The second set of verses is found in Matthew.

The term Day of the Lord is the final day of the present age. Jesus explains the parable of the weeds and it again helps clarify what happens at the end of this age.

Matthew 13:36-43, "Then he left the crowd and went into the house. His disciples came to him and said, "Explain to us the parable of the weeds in the field." He answered, "The one who sowed the good seed is the Son of Man. The field is the world, and the good seed stands for the sons of the kingdom. The weeds are the sons of the evil one, and the enemy who sows them is the devil. **The harvest is the end of** the age, and the harvesters are angels. "As the weeds are pulled up and burned in the fire, so it will be at the end of the age. The Son of Man will send out his angels, and they will weed out of his kingdom everything that causes sin and all who do evil. **They will throw them into the fiery furnace,** where **there will be weeping and gnashing of teeth.** Then the righteous will shine like the sun in the kingdom of their Father. He who has ears, let him hear."

This Scripture tells us the harvest is on the last day of this age. Those who are not in Christ are to be judged and punished. Then Christ warned whoever has an ear, let them hear! Again, Christ's own words seem to indicate which way we should view the thousand years. The key here is that we know the next major event is the second coming of Christ and that is sufficient. The rest will be revealed and understood after God executes His plan for us.

Chapter 21 - gives us a glimpse of our future home. We know it will defy imagination. It will be a place of no tears, no pain, no death, and no curse of time. It is for those who overcome in Christ.

Chapter 22 - The curse is removed. "Behold I am coming soon. All who wish may come and take the free gift of the water of life." This chapter ends with a warning not to add or take away from the Word of God.

Visual Review of History and Revelation

1793 -1815 A.D.	1st Bowl - Holy Roman Catholic Church power removed
1793 -1815 A.D.	2nd Bowl - England destroy Papal Naval Forces
1793 -1815 A.D.	3rd Bowl - Central Europe freed form the Beast
1793 -1815 A.D.	4th Bowl - Napolean is identified as the leader
1793 - End of age	5th Bowl - Catholic Popes are given time to repent
1917 A.D	6th Bowl - Ottoman Empire collasped
Three (3) Anti-christian Forces 20th & 21st Century Identified	1-Roman Catholic Church until it changes from tradition-based belief to scripture based-belief 2- Islamic Nations 3- Communism (rises October 1917 as predicted)
1945 A.D	7th Bowl - Nuclear Age begins with its Curse
Unknown	7th Trumpet - Last Day of this present age.

THE RAPTURE

The word Rapture, when used by Christians, usually refers to an event all Christians are looking forward to unfolding in the future. However, this event comes with a variety of different understandings, expectations, and interpretations. There are two major interpretations in the church today. Depending on what end-time view you have learned will determine your usage and understanding of what the rapture means. Rapture is the term that is associated with the saints of God meeting the Lord in the air at the second coming of Christ. The difference in the interpretations is that some believe that the rapture is at the end of the present age and others believe that it is seven years before the end of the age with another or second return seven years later.

This created a dilemma for me. Only one view of the end times can be correct, causing me to have the following series of questions:

Is the rapture one stage or two?

Is the church here up until the end of this age?

Is there a secret rapture?

I am forced to consider all the arguments as equal until I am able to find the Achilles heel of an argument. Since the Bible is the only source of absolute truth, the different interpretations must be methodically compared to the whole of Scripture. A rule I learned, and have tried to be faithful to in this writing, is the warning of what is known as the Restoration Plea. The **Restoration Plea** basically states, "Speak where the Bible speaks and remain silent where the Bible is silent." There are things that God keeps secret, or is silent about. Deuteronomy 29:29:

> "The secret things belong to the LORD our God, but the things revealed belong to us and to our children forever, that we may follow all the words of this law."

With this as a guiding principle, Truth has to become obvious and, in this case, the actual verses must declare the truth before I can take a position. How do I get a real understanding and find truth? Stay true to the principles of the Restoration Plea until truth becomes obvious.

THE END OF TIME

This section started with a review of the key "end of the age, or world" verses.

1 Thessalonians 4:16:17: "For the Lord himself will come down from heaven, with a **loud** command, with the voice of the archangel and with the **trumpet call** of God, and the dead in Christ will rise first. After that, we who are still alive and are left will be caught up together with them in the clouds to meet the Lord in the air. And so we will be with the Lord forever."

This verse tells us that there is a **LOUD** command, an angel sounds the trumpet, the **DEAD** in Christ rise first, then those alive rise to meet Christ in the air.

1 Corinthians 15:51-52: "Listen, I tell you a mystery: We will not all sleep, but we will all be changed in a flash, in the twinkling of an eye, **at the last trumpet**. For the trumpet will sound, the dead will be raised imperishable, and we will be changed."

This verse tells us that the trumpet is the **Last Trumpet.** The Last trumpet is the same as the **SEVENTH TRUMPET** from Revelation.

Rev 1:7: "Look, he is coming with the clouds, and **every eye** will see him, …"

Every eye will see Him. This means Christ's return will be SEEN BY ALL.

2 Peter 3:10-13: "But the day of the Lord will come like a thief. The heavens will **disappear with a roar; …**"

The time will be **UNKNOWN** and there will be a **ROAR.**

Matthew 24:36-42: "No one knows about that day or hour, not even the angels in heaven, nor the Son, but **only the Father**. As it was in the **days of Noah**, so it will be at the coming of the Son of Man. For in the days before the flood, people were eating and drinking, marrying and giving in marriage, up to the day Noah entered the ark;

and they knew nothing about what would happen until the flood came and took them all away. That is how it will be at the coming of the Son of Man. Two men will be in the field; one will be taken and the other left. Two women will be grinding with a hand mill; one will be taken and the other left. "Therefore keep watch, because you do not know on what day your Lord will come."

These verses reveal a very important message that cannot be overstated. NO ONE KNOWS THE TIME OF THE LAST DAY, NOT THE ANGELS, NOT EVEN CHRIST, ONLY THE FATHER! Anyone who tries to set a date for the return of Christ is foolish. The second thing that these verses tell us is that people living at the end of the world will be living their lives doing normal and routine things such as eating, drinking, and marrying. Like the days of Noah, they will be caught unprepared. The non-Christians are there to the end.

John 17:13-15: "I am coming to you now, but I say these things while I am still in the world, so that they may have the full measure of my joy within them. I have given them your word and the world has hated them, for they are not of the world any more than I am of the world. **My prayer is not that you take them out of the world** but that you protect them from the evil one."

Jesus' prayer is not to take his disciples or the church out of this world but to protect them from the evil one. **WE ARE NOT TO BE TAKEN OUT.**

Luke 19:11-13: "While they were listening to this, he went on to tell them a parable, because he was near Jerusalem and the people thought that the kingdom of God was going to appear at once. He [Jesus] said: "A man of noble birth went to a distant country to have himself appointed king and then to return. So he called ten of his servants and gave them ten minas. 'Put this money to work,' he said, 'until I come back.'"

The Parable of the Ten Minas is a parable about the return of Christ to set up the Kingdom of God. The Jewish people were confused. They wanted their Messiah to establish the Kingdom of God then so that they could come out from under the yoke of Roman power. Christ tells his servants that here is some money for you to invest until I come back. This indicates that we, his servants, are to invest wisely and **will be here when he returns.**

John 6:38-40: "For I have come down from heaven not to do my will but to do the will of him who sent me. And this is the will of him who sent me, that I shall lose none of all that he has given me, but raise them up at the last day. For my Father's will is that everyone who looks to the Son and believes in him shall have eternal life, **and I will raise him up at the last day."**

I think this verse does answer the question of whether the church is here to the last day. Everyone who puts their faith in Christ will have eternal life. This collective group is the church. **THE CHURCH CLEARLY IS RAISED UP ON THE LAST DAY.**

Matthew 13:47-50: "Once again, the kingdom of heaven is like a net that was let down into the lake and caught all kinds of fish. When it was full, the fishermen pulled it up on the shore. Then they sat down and collected the good fish in baskets, but threw the bad away. This is how it will be at the end of the age. **The angels will come and separate the wicked from the righteous** and throw them into the fiery furnace, where there will be weeping and gnashing of teeth.

Jesus' Parable of the Net tells us that both the **WICKED** and **RIGHTEOUS ARE THERE WHEN THE ANGELS COME.** This indicates the church is going to be here right up to the last day of the age.

Let's do a quick review: We know the return of Christ is LOUD (not secret), the trumpet sounds, the DEAD in Christ rise first, followed by those Christians who are alive. The Christians meet Christ in the air. The trumpet is the seventh or last trumpet.

Scripture states that, when Christ returns, EVERY EYE will see Him (not secret or invisible). The time is to be UNKNOWN and the heavens will disappear on the DAY OF THE LORD with a ROAR. Christ tells us that NO ONE KNOWS THE TIME OF THE LAST DAY EXCEPT GOD THE FATHER.

People will be living their lives doing routine and normal things when the end shall fall upon them on the last day at the return of Christ. Like the days of Noah, they will be caught by surprise. Jesus specifically prayed that the church not be taken out early, but rather protected from the evil one. Jesus then shared the parable of the Ten Minas. Here he teaches us to invest and work hard until he returns. Christ's return is on the last day of this age. This indicates that the CHURCH is present on earth to the LAST DAY. In the Gospel of John, Jesus tells His disciplines that whomever looks to the Son and believes shall have eternal life, and I WILL RAISE HIM UP ON THE LAST

The Final Trumpet

DAY. THIS MEANS **JESUS WILL RAISE THE CHURCH UP ON THE LAST DAY OF THIS AGE!** The parable of the Net says the angels come and separate the wicked from the righteous. We know the angels come for judgment on the **LAST DAY**. When Jesus appears, his angels are with Him in mass and they are referred to as **REAPERS!**

I believe, based on what Scripture indicates, the answer to the questions are as follows:

Is the rapture one stage or two? **ONE**
Is the church here up to the end of this age? **YES**
Is there a secret rapture? **NO**

There are a host of additional problems associated with a secret rapture followed by a seven year period before Christ returns and the end of the world happens. If there were a secret rapture, then those remaining behind know the exact date of the LAST DAY. This date, according to the Bible, is reserved for God alone; not even Jesus knows. Yet, everyone left behind would now know the date of the last day. *IT WOULD BE SEVEN YEARS FROM THE DAY THE CHURCH DISAPPEARED!* The most popular last day teaching tells us that there is a seven year great tribulation upon the earth. The church is removed. At the end of seven years Christ returns. Those left behind will witness millions suddenly vanish. They would now be able to know when Christ's second coming would happen. Scripture states people will be like those during Noah's day. They had no clue until destruction fell upon them. Again, one can be true.

A benefit to discovering a position's Achilles heel is that one does not have to waste time reviewing every detail that is attached to it. There may be some parts of it that are based on true concepts; however, this secret rapture theory has a fatal flaw. The fatal flaw is that it does not match up to Scripture. It requires one to undo the 70th week prophecy that Christ specifically fulfilled on time as shown in detail earlier in this writing. If this secret rapture was a plot of the Beast (Papacy) from the 16th Century then it was done for a reason. Francisco Ribera (1537-1591), a Catholic professor at Salmanca, is credited with the creation of an interpretation that John the Apostle only foresaw events of the near future and of the final things at the end of the world. He defined the Antichrist as a future individual who would rise in the end times just before the return of Christ. This has become the major view of prophecy during the 20th Century. Its conditions all those in the church who hear and believe it, to accept as God's will that evil is going to rise. Things are going to go downhill for the church of God.

However, believing this view, Christians are not to worry, as they will leave before the ANTICHRIST appears. This is incredible - so easy to like. There is no responsibility, no cross to bear, it requires no effort from us, as it is seemingly hopeless, what can we do? (I oppose evil then I might actually be out of God's will.) Who authors such a deception? The beast works for whom? The secret rapture theory rose up during the 19th Century at the same time higher criticism made its entrance. Evolution, and now these other excellently implemented deceptions, have the body of Christ, the church, in a state of confusion with misdirection causing the church to be ineffective in its mission.

Why rewrite the end of the world? The time of the Beast's (Papacy) power is over. Why study prophecy? Because what beliefs are held collectively by the body of Christ affect the Church's response to evil, to moral decay, to working hard for Christ, etc. Previously, I stated "The Biblical view is that which God does is always vitally related to what MAN DOES!" Listen to what this verse says:

> 2 Peter 3:10-13, "But the day of the Lord will come like a thief. The heavens will disappear with a roar; the elements will be destroyed by fire, and the earth and everything in it will be laid bare. Since everything will be destroyed in this way, what kind of people ought you to be? **You ought to live holy and godly lives as you look forward to the day of God and speed its coming.** That day will bring about the destruction of the heavens by fire, and the elements will melt in the heat. But in keeping with his promise we are looking forward to a new heaven and a new earth, the home of righteousness."

In the middle of these verses is the answer. Christians are to live holy and Godly lives as we look forward to the day of the God and **SPEED ITS COMING!** This means to obey God and his commands. Obey his primary command, go and make disciples! The Bible tells us in Matthew 16:18: "And I tell you that you are Peter, and on this rock I will build my church, and the gates of Hades will not overcome it." This is such a smart deception. Satan knows that if the church goes out and makes disciples like it should, it will shorten his time. Why study Prophecy? So that our focus, energy, priorities, resources, and time are all made available in order that the church can work together to shorten the time until the day Christ returns and we enter into our new home.

TRUTH VERSUS NOT EXACTLY

Jesus returns on the last day of this age. These coming events will be at the last (7th) trumpet – loud and visible to all. The dead rise first, the church will meet Him in the air. The angels come to reap. Only God the Father knows the time. It will be like the days of Noah.
LAST DAY

OR
7 YEARS?
Or, Jesus returns seven years prior, thus necessitating two returns. First return would be the secret rapture of the church with the Holy Spirit. Everyone else who is left behind would know the date of the second coming of Christ. One problem: Scripture states only the Father knows. Here is the problem with the Law of Non-Contradiction: Both cannot be correct. The Restoration Plea tells us to look at Scripture and, if it says something clearly, accept it and believe it. If it does not speak clearly, or is silent, do not add or speculate. Scripture is clear as to what will transpire on the last day of the world. Christians must have the correct understanding of the future and their God-given mission to be truly effective. Believe only what Scripture has told us.

Numbers do not validate Truth. In the business world, we are constantly told to be team players and that it is important to show up at work with an attitude that fits the culture. However, there is a concern when everyone agrees with those in charge. A prime example used to teach people the dangers of what is known as "Group Think" is the Challenger disaster. Engineers suspected complications, and informed NASA management with a launch below a certain temperature. We now know that they were persuaded to be team players by management, and the results are history. This also happens in the church world. At seminary, many future ministers are trained in their denomination's doctrines, beliefs, theology, and interpretations. It is logical that the leadership would want conformity and not chaos throughout their denomination and churches. However, the downside is the possibility of "Spiritual Group Think."

TRUTH VERSUS NOT EXACTLY

It may be hard to unlearn the secret rapture theory if you have been indoctrinated with this. Earlier in this writing, I shared how devastated I was to learn that so much of what I had been taught was either a lie or based on some untruth or partial truth. However, today I am not under the control of those lies, partial truths, and/or outright deceptions. It is hard to admit that I believed something that had not been true. Realize this secret rapture theory was packaged and delivered by the master of deception himself. Even some in the church have unknowingly aided.

The same as "In the Day's of Noah"

If you are a non-believer right now, you must understand that there is no secret rapture. When Christ appears with His armies on the last day at the sounding of the seventh trumpet, that is it – no second chance, no time to change sides. The angels will come and, just as in the days of Noah, their destruction will be complete. They did not have a second chance to reconsider. If you die without accepting Christ as your Savior, you have locked your fate forever. As a believer, this should motivate us to live Godly lives and be a testimony to this world. We have been commanded by Jesus to love God with all our hearts and others as ourselves. Do we love enough to share the **eternal gift of life** with every fellow man and woman that we have a relationship with whom God has strategically placed in our lives?

COMPLETE REVIEW OF TRIBULATION

The word **"thlipsis"** (number 2347 in Strong's Concordance), the word that is translated "**tribulation in MATTHEW 24:21 and Revelation 7:14**," is translated "tribulation, affliction, anguish, persecution, burdened and trouble. Every text in which this word is used will be reviewed.

Tribulations Against the JEWS (5 References)

1-Mat 24:21 For then shall be **great tribulation,** such as was not since the beginning of the world to this time, no, nor ever shall be. Remember this answers the first question they asked Jesus about the temple.

2-Mat 24:29 Immediately after **the tribulation** of those days shall the sun be darkened, and the moon shall not give her light, and the stars shall fall from heaven, and the powers of the heavens shall be shaken:

3-Mark 13:19 because those will be days of **distress** unequaled from the beginning, when God created the world, until now—and never to be equaled again.

4-Mark 13:24 But in those days, following that **distress**, the sun will be darkened, and the moon will not give its light;

5-Luke 21:23 How dreadful it will be in those days for pregnant women and nursing mothers! There will be great **distress** in the land and wrath against this people.Luke 21:24 And they shall fall by the edge of the sword, and shall be led away captive into all nations: and Jerusalem shall be trodden down of the

Gentiles, until the times of the Gentiles be fulfilled.

All of this came to pass in 70 A.D. This is all in the PAST!

Tribulation Against Christians (36 References)

1-John 16:33 These things I have spoken unto you, that in me ye might have peace. In the world ye shall have **tribulation:** but be of good cheer; I have overcome the world.

2-Acts 14:22 Confirming the souls of the disciples, and exhorting them to continue in the faith, and that we must through much **tribulation** enter into the kingdom of God.

3-Rom 5:3 And not only so, but we glory in **tribulations** also: knowing that tribulation worketh patience;

4-Rom 8:35-37 Who shall separate us from the love of Christ? shall **tribulation,** or distress, or persecution, or famine, or nakedness, or peril, or sword? As it is written, For thy sake we are killed all the day long; we are accounted as sheep for the slaughter. Nay, in all these things we are more than conquerors through him that loved us.

5-Rom 12:12 Rejoicing in hope; patient in **tribulation**; continuing instant in prayer; 6-2 Cor 7:4 Great is my boldness of speech toward you, great is my glorying of you: I am filled with comfort, I am exceeding joyful in all our **tribulation**.

7-Eph 3:13 Wherefore I desire that ye faint not at my **tribulations** for you, which is your glory.8-2 Thess 1:4 So that we ourselves glory in you in the churches of God for your patience and faith in all your persecutions and **tribulations** that ye endure:

9-2 Cor 1:4 Who comforteth us in all our **tribulation**, that we may be able to comfort them which are in any **trouble,** by the comfort wherewith we ourselves are comforted of God.

10-Mat 13:21 Yet hath he not root in himself, but dureth for a while: for when **tribulation** or persecution ariseth because of the word, by and by he is offended.

11-Mat 24:9 Then shall they deliver you up to be **afflicted**, and shall kill you: and ye shall be hated of all nations for my name's sake.

12-Mark 4:17 And have no root in themselves, and so endure but for a time: afterward, when **affliction or persecution** ariseth for the word's sake, immediately they are offended.

13-Heb 10:33 Partly, whilst ye were made a gazing stock both by reproaches and **afflictions**; and partly, whilst ye became companions of them that were so used.

14-2 Cor 8:2 How that in a great trial of **affliction** the abundance of their joy and their deep poverty abounded unto the riches of their liberality.

15-1 Thess 1:6 And ye became followers of us, and of the Lord, having received the word in much **affliction,** with joy of the Holy Ghost:

16-1 Thess 3:3 That no man should be moved by these **afflictions:** for yourselves know that we are appointed thereunto.

17-2 Cor 4:17 For our light **affliction,** which is but for a moment, worketh for us a far more exceeding and eternal weight of glory;

18-2 Cor 2:4 For out of much **affliction** and anguish of heart I wrote unto you with many tears; not that ye should be grieved, but that ye might know the love which I have more abundantly unto you

19-2 Cor 6:4 But in all things approving ourselves as the ministers of God, in much patience, in **afflictions**, in necessities, in distresses,

The Final Trumpet

20-2 Cor 6:5 In stripes, in imprisonments, in tumults, in labours, in watchings, in fastings;

21-Acts 20:23 Save that the Holy Ghost witnesseth in every city, saying that bonds and **afflictions** abide me.

22-Col 1:24 Who now rejoice in my sufferings for you, and fill up that which is behind of the **afflictions** of Christ in my flesh for his body's sake, which is the church:

23-1 Thess 3:7 Therefore, brethren, we were comforted over you in all our **affliction** and distress by your faith:

24-1 Thess 3:8 For now we live, if ye stand fast in the Lord.

25-Phil 1:16 The one preach Christ of contention, not sincerely, supposing to add **affliction** to my bonds:

26-Phil 4:14 Notwithstanding ye have well done, that ye did communicate with my **affliction.**

Thlipsis is also translated "trouble" in:

27-2 Cor 1:8 For we would not, brethren, have you ignorant of our **trouble** which came to us in Asia, that we were pressed out of measure, above strength, insomuch that we despaired even of life:

Thlipsis is also translated "persecution" in:

28-Acts 11:19 Now they which were scattered abroad upon the **persecution** that arose about Stephen travelled as far as Phenice, and Cyprus, and Antioch, preaching the word to none but unto the Jews only.

29-Rev 1:9 I John, who also am your brother, and companion in **tribulation**, and in the kingdom and patience of Jesus Christ, was in the isle that is called Patmos, for the word of God, and for the testimony of Jesus Christ.

30-Rev 7:14 And I said unto him, Sir, thou knowest. And he said to me, These are they which came out of **great tribulation,** and have washed their robes, and made them white in the blood of the Lamb.

Other verses which do not bear directly but mentioned for the sake of completeness:

31-2 Cor 8:13 For I mean not that other men be eased, and ye **burdened:**

32-James 1:27 Pure religion and undefiled before God and the Father is this, To visit the fatherless and widows in their **affliction,** and to keep himself unspotted from the world.

33-Acts 7:10 And delivered him out of all his **afflictions,** and gave him favour and wisdom in the sight of Pharaoh king of Egypt; and he made him governor over Egypt and all his house.

34-Acts 7:11 Now there came a dearth over all the land of Egypt and Chanaan, and great **affliction:** and our fathers found no sustenance.

35-John 16:21 A woman when she is in travail hath sorrow, because her hour is come: but as soon as she is delivered of the child, she remembereth no more the **anguish,** for joy that a man is born into the world.

36-1 Cor 7:28 But and if thou marry, thou hast not sinned; and if a virgin marry, she hath not sinned. Nevertheless such shall have **trouble** in the flesh: but I *spare you.*

Tribulation Against The Wicked (3)

1-Rom 2:9 **Tribulation** and anguish, upon every soul of man that doeth evil, of the Jew first, and also of the Gentile;

2-2 Thess 1:6 Seeing it is a righteous thing with God to recompense **tribulation** to them that trouble you;

3-Rev 2:22 Behold, I will cast her into a bed, and them that commit adultery with her into **great tribulation**, except they repent of their deeds.

SUMMARY OF TRIBULATION USAGE

THLIPSIS is used over forty times in Scripture. Five references are to the great distress or great tribulation that came upon the Jews and Jerusalem in 70 A.D. Was there a specific period of time tied to this event? Was the great tribulation on the Jews an event or time period? Event, as no length is provided in any direct reference to this great tribulation.

Over thirty references to tribulation refer to Believers because of their **stand for CHRIST**. In these references **NOT ONE** of them is speaking of a **specific period** of time, but of tribulation **IN GENERAL!** Revelation 7:14 the question is the same. Is there a specific period of time or an event? Was the great tribulation mentioned here tied to any time specific period? Again, no length is provided.

Three references of tribulation are against the wicked. One reference to the wicked is that they will suffer great tribulation if they do not repent. Is the great tribulation meant here as a period of time for the wicked to be punished? Or simply they will get great tribulation for being evil if they do not repent! The second reading requires no elaboration; it states what is said clearly by the author.

Review the forty plus verses in their context and then answer the next question. Is the great tribulation, affliction, distress, trouble, persecution, anguish, or burden used in any verse in conjunction with a seven-year time period prior to the return of Christ? No.

Then what is the purpose of telling us about tribulation?

For the Jew living near 70 A.D.: this was their fate they had chosen. God was announcing to them their destiny, unless they repented. A single event would fall on them within one generation of the death of Christ. Jesus foretold this event and it is part of recorded history. This is the Great Tribulation against the Jews. This is different than the great tribulation mentioned concerning the believer in Revelation.

For the wicked: this is their fate unless they repent. The wicked are warned that those who do evil against the church during the great tribulation will suffer greatly. The church started at Pentecost and is here till the last day. The great tribulation is the possible time that Christians living in this world are open to persecution by the wicked.

For the Believer: we are told that we will suffer, have tribulation in this life, with the possibility of even death. God tells us so that when tribulations happen we are prepared for them even though no one likes to go through ordeals that test our faith and commitment.

1 Thess 3:3 That no man should be moved by these **afflictions:** for yourselves know that we are appointed thereunto.

1 Thess 3:4 For verily, when we were with you, we told you before that we should suffer **tribulation**; even as it came to pass, and ye know.

We are appointed to tribulations. Throughout history there has been and they will continue up until THAT DAY, the end of the age. This is the answer to what is meant by the great tribulation. The key is understanding how it is used and in what content to the whole of Scripture.

Revelation 7:14, becomes clear when read in its context and in relation to the whole of Scripture. The great tribulation in Revelation is the time period from Pentecost to the last day when Christ returns.

The great tribulation in Matthew 24:21 is an event upon the Jew by the Romans. They have two distinct messages. Matthew was for the Jews in 70 A.D. and Revelation was for the church throughout history.

ANTICHRIST OR ANTICHRISTS

There are two key sections in Scripture that reveal to us who is antichrist. This is the last hour and many antichrists have come already. Who are these antichrists? They were part of the first century church, but not really true believers. How do you spot them? They deny that Jesus is the Christ. They deny that Jesus came in the flesh. Our generation has been taught that in the last days a super Antichrist is coming. This is some powerful leader in the future of some one world government or unified Europe. The following Scriptures clearly appear not to support this concept.

I JOHN 2:13-27

Warning Against Antichrists is found in **I John 2:13-27** which states: "Dear children, this is the last hour; and as you have heard that the **antichrist** is coming, even now many **antichrists** have come. This is how we know it is the last hour. They went out from us, but they did not really belong to us. For if they had belonged to us, they would have remained with us; but their going showed that none of them belonged to us. But you have an anointing from the Holy One, and all of you know the truth. I do not write to you because you do not know the truth, but because you do know it and because no lie comes from the truth. Who is the liar? It is the man who denies that Jesus is the Christ. Such a man is the **antichrist**—he denies the Father and the Son. No one who denies the Son has the Father; whoever acknowledges the Son has the Father also. See that what you have heard from the beginning remains in you. If it does, you also will remain in the Son and in the Father. And this is what he promised us—even eternal life. I am writing these things to you about those who are trying to lead you astray. As for you, the anointing you received from him remains in you, and you do not need anyone to teach you. But as his anointing teaches you about all things and as that anointing is real, not counterfeit—just as it has taught you, remain in him."

> # I JOHN 4:1-7
>
> We are told to test the spirits **I John 4:1-7** states: "Dear friends, do not believe every spirit, but test the spirits to see whether they are from God, because many false prophets have gone out into the world. This is how you can recognize the Spirit of God: Every spirit that acknowledges that Jesus Christ has come in the flesh is from God, but every spirit that does not acknowledge Jesus is not from God. This is the spirit of the antichrist, which you have heard is coming and even now is already in the world. You, dear children, are from God and have overcome them, because the one who is in you is greater than the one who is in the world. They are from the world and therefore speak from the viewpoint of the world, and the world listens to them. We are from God, and whoever knows God listens to us; but whoever is not from God does not listen to us. This is how we recognize the Spirit of truth and the spirit of falsehood. Many deceivers, who do not acknowledge Jesus Christ as coming in the flesh, have gone out into the world. Any such person is the deceiver and the **antichrist.** Watch out that you do not lose what you have worked for, but that you may be rewarded fully.

    H.Gratten Guinness, England's greatest teacher of Bible prophecy, wrote this as a warning, "A wide distinction exists and should be recognized between students and expositors of the Word and Works of God who humbly, soberly and reverently search into the facts of Nature and Scripture, of providence and prophecy, reach conclusions which sanctified common sense can approve, and speculators, who, running away with isolated and mysterious expressions, indulge in imaginations of their own and become prophets, instead of students of divine prophecy."

    As I read book after book about prophecy covering the book of Revelation, there was no limit to the speculation and possible scenarios that have been presented. I started with the most popular: Dispensationalism. This moves the 70th Week a final seven-year period, to the end of the age. The Law of Non-Contradiction does not allow these conflicting ideas to both be true. Either what Jesus stated was true, or man's interpretation was true. Jesus said no one knows the exact final date, except God the Father. This is the same as choosing between real scientific laws or evolutionary theories of men. The choice is easy to make. I choose Scripture and Christ over anything else.

    If the multitudes in white robes from chapter seven did not come from a seven-year period, then where? I looked for the obvious. Scripture said they were from every nation, tribe, people and language, standing before the throne and in front of the Lamb. Every means all. All means all of the saved. It must include both Jew and Gentile. This meant the Great Tribulation had to cover a period that would include all the saints from the Church. This translated, or drove, the great tribulation to cover from the beginning of the Church (Pentecost) to the end of the age (return of Christ).

My next challenging concept was the Millennium. Scripture states that the earth and heavens are consumed in a great roar on the last day at the return of Christ. Standard interpretation of the Millennium revolved around two major choices. The first, and dominant, was that the Millennium would be an actual 1000 year reign of Christ on earth after the second coming. The other was that everything was symbolic in the book of Revelation. It is flawed theology to spiritualize or turn everything into some symbolic message. What God speaks in clear terms needs to be received as such. What messages have been given to us, like parts of Revelation, for the purpose of showing the sovereign control of history by God are to be interpreted in light of fulfillment in history. Prophecy was given cloaked by God because it was for the saints and would be understood only after it was fulfilled.

The first thing was to see if a same term was used in Scripture with different meaning. As you read, the term has been used not to mean one thousand. The thousand years here is symbolic. In Bible usage, one thousand is a round, indefinite number. This caused me to examine Revelation, chapter 20 in a whole new light. Based on the assumption that Revelation was provided as a roadmap to the end of this age, I started looking at Revelation as providing a sequential timeline. Reading the context and comparing it to recorded history that God had allowed to happen I began to see how the battle between Satan and God played out in this world and the Church's history. As you read earlier showing each time Satan was limited the Church grew. The first time was the elevation of Christianity as the Empire's official religion followed by the period known as the Rise of Christianity. The second time was the Reformation, followed by the Great Awakenings and world-wide missionary movements. The Trumpets, Seals, and Bowls are identified as historical events in real history that are matched to what is revealed in Revelation. The 7th Bowl was not identified in any of the books that I had collected. However, I gave due consideration to the many warnings about looking at prophecy for the purpose of playing prophet. I knew looking forward was going to be a waste of time since God did not give us Revelation for that purpose. I then focused back into history and began looking for a match. I have put into this book what I believed would be the 7th Bowl based on the history that has happened. The dawn of the nuclear age is a major milestone in the history of man. It appeared to fit the symbolism that was provided. This means that all has been fulfilled and we wait for one event.

FINAL REVIEW

In summary, I needed to have all of my questions answered from scripture in a simple manner. Most of the books I had read, or speakers I had heard, on Revelation left me more confused as to where the presenting author or theologian obtained the information proffered. It appeared to be pulled out of scripture by taking a verse here, another verse there, and then building an elaborate and complex interpretation. The worst part was that I did not want to speak up for fear of looking stupid. I later found out that just about everyone I polled was just as bewildered. We comforted ourselves by believing the words of the experts, "Revelation is for the really mature and has the deep things of God which are hidden from most." This was not exactly true. In essence, you have just read "Revelation for Dummies."

Let's do a review:

1. **What are the first four empires in Daniel's prophecy?** Babylon, Medo-Persia, Greece and Rome
2. **During what empire would the Kingdom of God be established?** According to the Bible, it would appear during the Roman. However, this meant after 63 B.C. but before the collapse of Rome. Christ did come and fulfill this after 63 B.C.
3. **What is the 70-Week Prophecy?** It is a prophecy that reveals when God chose for the Messiah of this world to start His three-and-one-half year ministry. It would begin at the end of the sixty-nine weeks.
4. **What event according to scripture started the 70-Week Prophecy?** In 457 B.C., Artaxerxes I issued a decree to Ezra to rebuild the city of Jerusalem and its walls. The certainty of which date is correct was driven by knowing the date of Christ's death on the cross a historical date and fact of history.
5. **What happens to the Messiah during the 70th Week?** He was cut-off in the middle as foretold. After three-and-one-half years of ministry, He was crucified.
6. **The last half of the 70th Week was for what purpose?** The Gospel, or Good News, would be taken to the Jew first.
7. **Christ is asked two questions by the disciples when they were sitting on the Mount of Olives. What were they?**
Matthew 24:1-3, "Jesus left the **temple** and was walking away when his disciples came up to him to call his attention to its buildings. 'Do you see all these things?' he asked. '**I tell you the truth, not one stone here will be left on another; every one will be thrown down.**' As

Jesus was sitting on the Mount of Olives, the disciples came to him privately. 'Tell us,' they said, 'when will this happen, and what will be the sign of your coming and of the end of the age?'"

- The first and primary question that Jesus addressed was when the destruction of the temple would happen. He tells them that not one stone would be left on another.
- The second question was "What would be the sign of your coming and the end of the age?"

8. **When would the destruction of the temple happen?** Christ said it would be within one generation, or forty years. We know that it was destroyed within one generation in 70 A.D.
9. **Did wars and rumors of war come as Christ said to Rome?** Yes, even though, when Christ predicts wars and rumors of wars, Rome was experiencing peace at that time.
10. **Did Famines and Earthquakes come as Christ predicted?** Yes, it is recorded history.
11. **Did persecution & death come to those called Christians?** Yes, again. This is well documented in history.
12. **What is meant by the term "Abomination of Desolation"?** Luke 21:20-21, "A time is coming when you will see armies surround Jerusalem. Then you will know that it will soon be destroyed. Those who are in Judea should then escape to the mountains. Those in the city should get out. Those in the country should not enter the city." Daniel 9:26 told us it would be Roman armies and they would surround Jerusalem. The Abomination of Desolation is simply when Roman armies surround Jerusalem, then it is time to flee. This happened in 65 A.D. and the Christians did flee Judea and they were spared.
13. **What is meant by "The Great Tribulation" in Matthew 24?** Matthew 24:21-24, "For then there will be **great distress**, unequaled from the beginning of the world until now—and never to be equaled again. For then there will be **great tribulation** (affliction, distress, and oppression) such as has not been from the beginning of the world until now—no, and never will be [again]. If those days had not been **cut short, no one would survive**, but for the sake of the elect those days will be shortened. They will fall by the sword and will be taken as **prisoners to all the nations.** Jerusalem will be trampled on **by the Gentiles** until the times of the Gentiles are fulfilled." It is simply a gentile and we know Roman army that surround the Holy city of Jerusalem. It was the destruction of the Jews as recorded in history.

The Final Trumpet

14. **What will be the sign of the return of Christ?** Christ will appear in the sky with his armies.
15. **When will this happen?** No one knows the date - not even Christ, only the Father does. Avoid all date setters.
16. **Who is the book of Revelation written to?** The Church
17. **When was Revelation written?** 95 A.D.
18. **What verse provides the outline for the book of Revelation?** Revelation 1:19 provides this key information. Chapters one through three were recent past for John the writer. Chapters four and five were the present. Chapters six to twenty-two are in John's future.
19. **Who are the Four Horsemen of Revelation?** They are the first four seals. They represent what God predicts will happen to Rome.
20. **What are the seals found in Revelation?** Prophetic events are predicted. They then become understood as God's fulfillment in history is unfolded. They are provided to give the Church hope as it struggles forward.
21. **Who are the first four seals directed toward?** The Roman Empire
22. **Who are the 144,000?** They symbolize the Jews who would be the first fruits as clearly predicted. The Gospel was to go to the Jew first, then to the Gentile.
23. **Who are The Great Multitude in Chapter Seven?** They are the believers from the Church age.
24. **How long is the Church age?** The Day of Pentecost began the Church and the return of Christ will end the Church age.
25. **What are the Seven Trumpets?** The first four trumpets reveal the end of Rome's Western Empire, which then enters what is known in history as "The Dark Ages" in 476 A.D. The fifth trumpet is the collapse of the Roman Southern Empire and the Rise of Islam. The sixth trumpet is the destruction of Rome's Eastern Empire known as the Byzantine Empire in 1453 A.D. It also included the rise of the Ottoman Empire. The Seventh and Final Trumpet is yet to sound.
26. **Who is the Revived Roman Power?** When the Western Empire fell, it made way for the rise of a false power seated on the same seven hills in Rome, otherwise known as the Holy Roman Catholic Church.
27. **How long was the Holy Roman Catholic Church to have power?** 1,260 Years
28. **When did this prophecy start its fulfillment?** The Bishop of Rome is elevated above all other Bishops in 533 A.D. This caused a split in the Church.
29. **When did the Holy Roman Catholic Church's reign of power end?** In 1793, when Napoleon began his invasions.

30. **Who is clearly identified as The Beast with two different faces?** The Holy Roman Catholic Church.
31. **Is the Holy Roman Catholic Church still The Beast?** No, prophecy clearly states that it would lose its power and reemerge as an unrepentant hierarchy. In 1815, the Congress at Vienna attempted to restore the old order but the 380 principalities would never be assembled again. In 1870, Italy provided the Vatican to the Holy Roman Church.
32. **How long was the time of the Beast's power?** 1,260 Years (533 – 1793 A.D.)
33. **What was the Mark of The Beast?** At the height of the Beast's power no one could buy or sell, own property, etc. without paying allegiance to the popes.
34. **What does 666 mean?** 666 – The earliest solution to the meaning of the number was proposed by Irenaeus in the second century. He believed it to be the name LATEINOS [Greek for Latin]. Since the fourth kingdom was Rome, then the beast would be a Latin church in a Latin world. Dr. More reminds us, "They latinize everything: mass, prayers, hymns, litanies, canons, decretals, and bulls are conceived in Latin." In the Hebrew language, "Roman" happens to equal 666. The Holy Roman Catholic Church's calling card was definitely Latin and the Apostle John's prophecy has most certainly come true and clearly points to the Catholic Church; the Revived Rome.
35. **What are the Seven Bowls?** The first five bowls are poured out onto The Beast. They bring about a major reduction of the Beast's power. The sixth bowl predicts the end of the Ottoman Empire in 1917, and the three major ideologies that would struggle during the remainder of the 20th & 21st Centuries. The seventh bowl predicted an event that would upset the balance of power that has existed until the beginning of the Nuclear Age with its curse of political instability and potential randomness of terrorism.
36. **What is meant by Armageddon?** It is a symbolic term that is used to draw attention to the eventual exposure and coming defeat of all bankrupt philosophies and false religions by Christ at His return.
37. **What is the Millennium?** It is meant to be taken symbolically and is an indefinite length of time. Chapter 20 of Revelation shows the sequence of the Church's history in a mighty battle with Satan.
38. **What happens to the Church when Satan is thrown into the Abyss (Rev 20)?** The Church overthrew the pagan religions and becomes Rome's official religion.

The Final Trumpet

39. **What happens to the Church when Satan is released from the Abyss (Rev 20)?** Satan uses the Beast to attack the true believers. Millions of believers are martyred by the Beast.
40. **What happens when Satan is once again in prison (Rev 20)?** The Church enters the Reformation, followed by the Great Awakening, world-wide missionary movements, etc.
41. **What happens when Satan is released from prison (Rev 20)?** Satan begins a multiple front attack of deception. First from within the church came Higher Criticism. Second from the defense of the Beast would be a new deceptive interpretation of the Revelation. This interpretation would be completely opposite of what the Reformers and the Church had believed for centuries. It would take the 70th Week and put a gap between the 69th and 70th week. It would sell to Christians that evil would rise up and overtake all. The church had nothing to fear because the deception promised that when the Antichrist came the Church would be secretly raptured. The third was a brilliant attack on Genesis by Satan. An ex-theology student named Darwin would begin what every child today is being indoctrinated with by schools world-wide evolution for the first time removed God as the Creator in the eyes of most. This fueled the rise of Marxism and Communism.
42. **What is the New Jerusalem?** It is going to be our new home someday.
43. **What happens at the 7th and Final Trumpet?** I Thessalonians 4:16:17: "For the Lord himself will come down from heaven, with a **loud** command, with the voice of the archangel and with the **trumpet call** of God, and the dead in Christ will rise first. After that, we who are still alive and are left will be caught up together with them in the clouds to meet the Lord in the air. And so we will be with the Lord forever."

    This verse tells us that there is a **LOUD** command, an angel sounds the trumpet, the **DEAD** in Christ rise first, then those alive rise to meet Christ in the air. More happens. 1 Corinthians 15:51-52: "Listen, I tell you a mystery: We will not all sleep, but we will all be changed in a flash, in the twinkling of an eye, **at the last trumpet**. For the trumpet will sound, the dead will be raised imperishable, and we will be changed." We are to meet Christ and are changed. We will have new bodies.

    This verse tells us that the trumpet is the **Last Trumpet**. The Last trumpet is the same as the **SEVENTH TRUMPET** from Revelation.

44. **Who will see the return of Christ at His 2nd Advent?** Rev 1:7: "Look, he is coming with the clouds, and **every eye** will see him, …" Every eye will see Him. This means Christ's return will be SEEN BY ALL.

45. **When will Christ return?** Mathew 24:36-42: "No one knows about that day or hour, not even the angels in heaven, nor the Son, but **only the Father**. As it was in the **days of Noah**, so it will be at the coming of the Son of Man. For in the days before the flood, people were eating and drinking, marrying and giving in marriage, up to the day Noah entered the ark; and they knew nothing about what would happen until the flood came and took them all away. That is how it will be at the coming of the Son of Man. Two men will be in the field; one will be taken and the other left. Two women will be grinding with a hand mill; one will be taken and the other left. "Therefore keep watch, because you do not know on what day your Lord will come." These verses reveal a very important message that cannot be overstated. NO ONE KNOWS THE TIME OF THE LAST DAY, NOT THE ANGELS, NOT EVEN CHRIST, ONLY THE FATHER! Anyone who tries to set a date for the return of Christ is foolish. The second thing that these verses tell us is that people living at the end of the world will be living their lives doing normal and routine things such as eating, drinking, and marrying. Like the days of Noah, they will be caught unprepared. The non-Christians are there to the end.

46. **What about the Christians? Are we there to the end?** John 17:13-15: "I am coming to you now, but I say these things while I am still in the world, so that they may have the full measure of my joy within them. I have given them your word and the world has hated them, for they are not of the world any more than I am of the world. **My prayer is not that you take them out of the world** but that you protect them from the evil one." Jesus' prayer is not to take his disciples or the church out of this world but to protect them from the evil one. **WE ARE NOT TO BE TAKEN OUT.**

47. **What happens to the heavens at the return of Christ?** 2 Peter 3:10-13: "But the day of the Lord will come like a thief.
    The heavens will **disappear with a roar;** …"

This concludes our question and answer review. Following is another visual review.

THE BOOK OF REVELATION CONTAINS GOD'S FOREKNOWLEDGE.

	Visual Review of History and Prophecy
457 B.C.	Artaxerxes I Issues Decree to Ezra to rebuild Jerusulam; Starts Clock on 70 Week Propecy to when Messiah comes
408 B.C.	First 7 Weeks for Rebulding Jerusalem 7*7 = 49 Years
334 B.C.	Alexander The Great Invades Asia
285 B.C.	Old Testament Translation of Septuagint Version created as commanded by Ptolemy Philadelphus
63 B.C.	Rome Conquers Judea
4 B.C.	Birth of Christ
26 A.D.	End of 69 Weeks of 70th Week Prophecy (483 Years)
26 A.D.	Christ begins His Earthly Ministry at Age 30.
30 A.D.	First Half of 70th Week Prophecy Ends (3 1/2 Years)
30 A.D.	Christ Cut-off (Crucified) as Prophecy Predicted
33-34 A.D.	Second Half of 70th Week Prophecy Ends (3 1/2 Years)
33-34 A.D.	Gospel Goes First to the Jew as Foretold (3 1/2 Years)
34 A.D.	Philip went to Samaria and preached to Gentiles
60 A.D.	New Testament Complete Except for Book of Revelation
Pre-95 A.D.	Seven Churches established
95 A.D.	Apostle John receives Revelation and records it
Seals opened - Must Start Shortly - was as just 3 years 98 A.D.	
98 - 180 A.D.	1st Seal - White Horse - Peace of Rome
180 - 270 A.D.	2nd Seal - Red Horse - Civil War (80 emperors)
~200 - 303 A.D.	3rd Seal - Black Horse - Shortages & Famine
~250 - 303 A.D.	4th Seal - Pale Horse - Plague & Depopulation
303 - 313 A.D.	5th Seal - Era of Martyrs - Last Worldwide Persecution
313 - 460 A.D.	6th Seal - Rise of the Christian Church

HISTORY IS THE FULFILLMENT OF GOD'S FOREKNOWLEDGE

Visual Review of History and Prophecy

7th Seal opened which contains Seven Trumpets

410 A.D.	1st Trumpet - Goths lead by Alaric I sack Rome
429-455 A.D.	2nd Trumpet - King Geneseric - War at Sea
440 A.D.	3rd Trumpet - Attila the Hun - Rivers Turned Red
476 A.D.	4th Trumpet - Dark Ages Begin
612 A.D. & on	5th Trumpet - Rise of Islam - Conversion by Sword
1453 A.D	6th Trumpet - Rise of Turkish Empire - Last third falls

7th Trumpet delayed until Seven Plagues (bowls) Poured Out

THE BOOK IS OPENED - PREACHING STARTS REFORMATION

1455 A.D	Guttenberg Press
15-16th Century	Printing of Bibles In Common Languages
May 5, 1514	Papacy claims victory over heretics (true believers)
October 31, 1517	Luther nailed 95 Theses to the Wittenburg Church

Seven Plagues or Bowls are poured out

1793 -1815 A.D.	1st Bowl - Holy Roman Catholic Church power removed
1793 -1815 A.D.	2nd Bowl - England destroy Papal Naval Forces
1793 -1815 A.D.	3rd Bowl - Central Europe freed form the Beast
1793 -1815 A.D.	4th Bowl - Napolean is identified as the leader
1793 - End of age	5th Bowl - Catholic Popes are given time to repent
1917 A.D	6th Bowl - Ottoman Empire collasped
Three (3) Anti-christian Forces 20th & 21st Century Identified	1-Roman Catholic Church until it changes from tradition-based belief to scripture based-belief 2- Islamic Nations 3- Communism (rises October 1917 as predicted)
1945 A.D	7th Bowl - Nuclear Age begins with its Curse
UNKNOWN	7th Trumpet - Last Day of this present age

CONCLUSION

I have shared what has been laid on my heart. It troubles me to see people who have been led away from the truth. I wish there wasn't a battle for the minds and souls of every person who has ever lived. I wish that this world had no wars, no suffering, no pain, and no evil. I wish life was not so hard for so many. God in His infinite wisdom knows exactly what He is doing. It is virtually impossible for we humans to truly see the overall plan of God. We are asked by faith to trust God based on what He has revealed to us in His revelation to man, known as the Bible.

The true mark of divinity is the ability to predict the future. I got more than I could believe. First, I found out that the Old Testament foretold completely the history of empires rising and falling. It even described the battles, outcomes, and the players before they were born. Next, I found out that Christ's birth, destiny, death, and resurrection were all foretold in detail centuries prior to His arrival. Every event, His purpose, His mission, His death, and His resurrection were carefully shown in just over one hundred prophecies so that there could be no mistake as to who was the Messiah of this world. Even the time of His arrival was clearly revealed in the Seventy Weeks prophecy.

The Jews condemned Him as foretold. The Romans crucified Him as foretold.

After studying prophecy, I knew that the Bible had the **Seal of God** on it. I knew that it was the Truth. This may be your intervention. The Bible warns us in Matthew 7:22-23:

> "Many will say to me on that day, 'Lord, Lord, did we not prophesy in your name, and in your name drive out demons and perform many miracles?' Then I will tell them plainly, 'I never knew you. Away from me, you evildoers!'"

This is serious. Jesus tells people who thought they were in right standing that **HE NEVER KNEW THEM!**

Many are religious and do not know God. We need to meet the requirements that God has stated. No other religious activity will be acceptable. We must be sure what we are counting on is valid.

There is a lot of religious error in the world and I tested all that I was taught as it came, and will continue to do so.

My love of history, my love of the Scriptures, combined with a habit of reading all the books I could, helped me in my quest for understanding and truth. I am no historian. I just enjoy reading about history by the great historians. I am certainty no theologian. I just enjoy reading the writing of the great theologians of all ages. I am on the outside of the system and it allowed me to enter my search without the biases of indoctrination by the official religious doctrines of a particular view.

I knew that the documented occurrences in history could not be changed. I came to believe that God ensured that certain facts necessary for showing His Church that He was, and is, in complete control were recorded. As I laid Scripture sequentially against the world's history, it matched. We are in the debt of all who have gone on before us. The historians, the theologians, and many Christians have labored to preserve history for us. Our advantage is time. Everything up to the 7th bowl was found to be an historical event. The 7th Trumpet is the next event after the 7th bowl. We are waiting for this right now. It is the Return of Christ with His armies and angels. It is the day when the present Earth and Heavens are destroyed. It is the day when the Reapers of God (angels) separate those who go to the Great White Throne. It is the day when the dead in Christ rise first and we who are alive rise next to meet Christ in the air. It is the day of great distress for many who will be caught not ready, just as in the days of Noah. It is the day that those who are in Christ will go to the Judgment Seat of Christ. It is the day when the new heavens and earth are made. It is the day when we get our promised glorified bodies. It is the day when every tear is wiped away. It is the day when the final doom of Satan is accomplished and he is thrown into the Lake of Fire forever. It is the day that is coming as sure as the sun will rise tomorrow. It is a day for which to be prepared. Are you ready? I know one thing. I do not want what I Deserve. I Prefer His Glorious Grace.

> Everything has come to pass Exactly as foretold by God in His word. The Final Trumpet shall sound! **ARE YOU READY?**

GETTING READY

The best place to start to understand the Good News is in the book of Romans. Instead of evolution, God reveals that man's course has been devolution. The Apostle Paul opens his case by showing the unrighteousness of the Gentile world. Man started high-created in the image of God-then, because of sin, sank lower than the beasts. Man knew God, yet he turned from the truth. In Romans 1:20, God declares we are without excuse: "For since the creation of the world God's invisible qualities—his eternal power and divine nature—have been clearly seen, being understood from what has been made, so that men are without excuse." Yet, we chose not truth, but vain philosophies. I did not know God, as I had no religious upbringing. God responds to my attempt to escape in Romans 2:12-15, "All who sin apart from the law will also perish apart from the law, and all who sin under the law will be judged by the law. For it is not those who hear the law who are righteous in God's sight, but it is those who obey the law who will be declared righteous. Indeed, when Gentiles, who do not have the law, do by nature things required by the law, they are a law for themselves, even though they do not have the law, since they show that the requirements of the law are written on their hearts, their consciences also bearing witness, and their thoughts now accusing, now even defending them." Therefore, I have no excuse because God has written the laws on my heart and provided me with a conscience. What about all the religious folks who sin? The Apostle Paul deals with that exact issue next. If you are religious and have been taught religion, listen to what is in Romans 2:23-24: "You who brag about the law, do you dishonor God by breaking the law? As it is written: 'God's name is blasphemed among the Gentiles because of you.'" How many times has the religious person been caught doing the same as the non-religious, so much so that their actions make the non-religious not consider God? God comes right out and says if you know the law you are held to a higher standard. The Jews got the message. You had God in your presence, His laws. You had been blessed, and still you disobey. The Apostle drives home the final point that no one likes to hear, but everyone must. Roman 3:23, **"There is no difference, for all have sinned and fall short of the glory of God."** We are all the same, not one of us is any better or worse. I really did not need God to tell me that I missed the mark, I knew it. We are all basically sinners, racially condemned because of Adam, and guilty because we also sin daily. Romans 6:23: **"For the wages of sin is death."** That would be depressing if God had not provided a solution. Turning to Romans 3:21-25: "But now a righteousness from God, apart from law, has been made known, to which the Law and the Prophets testify. This righteousness from God comes through faith in Jesus Christ to all who believe. There is no difference, for all have sinned and fall short of the glory of God, and are justified freely by his grace through the redemption that came by Christ Jesus. God presented him as a sacrifice of atonement, through faith in his blood."

If I understood this correctly, I was completely and totally justified by God. I was guilty and condemned before God. I have been acquitted and declared righteous. How does this happen? This is critical. It is totally and completely an act of God. Justification is an act where God declares the believing sinner righteous in Christ on the basis of the finished work of Christ on the Cross. If I comprehend this correctly, God has imputed His righteousness into me. Salvation is justified by FAITH! We are justified by an act of God only! How do I appropriate my righteousness from God? By Faith! Too simple.

Nothing is one-hundred percent free, so what must I do? First, I needed to recognize that I was a sinner. I have met folks who thought they were okay. They felt they were basically good. What they meant was, we are better than the average individual. Sometimes, religion can give us a false sense that we are okay. However, it only matters what God says. Here is the test:

THE TEN COMMANDMENTS

1-"You shall have no other gods before me."
This means never putting God second. I failed.
2-"Thou shalt not have any graven image before me."
If a religion requires us to pray to hand-made items, this offends God.
3-"You shall not misuse the name of the LORD your God, for the LORD will not hold anyone guiltless who misuses his name."
Who has not done this?
4-"Remember the Sabbath day by keeping it holy."
We used to but, come on, it is the 21st Century.
5-"Honor your father and your mother."
Our culture promotes rebellion in our youth and disrespect for the elderly.
6-"You shall not murder."
Here is one I felt I had "passed" until Jesus spoke on it. He said if you ever had hate for someone, you were guilty of this one.
7-"You shall not commit adultery."
Jesus said if you look upon someone and lust for him or her, this is adultery.
8-"You shall not steal."
How many things do you need to steal to be considered a thief? One – I qualified as a thief, too.
9-"You shall not give false testimony against your neighbor."
How many lies does it take to be a liar? Again, just one.
10-"You shall not covet." Okay, ten for ten.

The Final Trumpet

So, what is the point? It only takes one infraction in our lifetime to be in need of God's offer! I recognized that I failed the test and needed God's offer. So, what do I get out of this deal?

According to God's Word in Romans, Chapter 5, seven blessings:

First, is **PEACE WITH GOD**. Non-believers are presently at enmity with God, whether they are aware of it or not. In fact, God is not even their father.

Second, We get **DIRECT ACCESS TO GOD**. What is meant by DIRECT? God tells us we have DIRECT access – no middlemen. Middlemen are better known as the **"BONDAGE BOYS,"** because they add requirements to be saved and to have access to GOD, with a price attached, which is control or some form of extraction of money.

Third, We get **HOPE.** This is probably the greatest gift. It is tied to the fact that GOD will no longer **REMEMBER** our sins. All of our sins are gone! This is Good News! The video is erased!

Fourth, We get a **Character Development Plan.** God will now use the issues and trials of life to work for us and not against us. Problems are coming, but God will use them for a different purpose. His Holy Spirit will indwell us and provide guidance and overcoming power.

Fifth, **God will pour His love into our hearts.** God will gives us a whole knew perspective with which to see the world, including a new attitude.

Sixth, **We get salvation from future wrath.**

Seventh, **We are reconciled back to God**. Atonement means reconciliation, or to be brought back into fellowship with God.

The rest of Chapter 5 of Romans discusses how the first Adam lost it all for us, and how the second Adam (Jesus) restored it, but with more.

Jesus was asked what must a man do to go to heaven? He must he born of the spirit, re-born again.

BONDAGE BOYS

This section is for those who are possibly re-born, but carry a heavy yoke of additional requirements never intended by God, or Christ. Millions of people have, in earnest, attempted to find fulfillment of deep and legitimate needs of the human spirit in church. The problem is that not all churches teach what is revealed in the Scriptures.

First clue: is there anything else that is equal to the Bible? If there is tradition, doctrines, books, or later revelations about Christ or God, then you are attending a place that is NOT EXACTLY correct. If you have been taught that you cannot understand the Bible without the official organization explaining it to you, then you are subject to being under their control and being put into bondage. God has clearly stated that He has given us the HOLY SPIRIT to lead us into all truth. I John 2:27 states: "As for you, the anointing [Holy Spirit] you received from him remains in you, and you do not need anyone to teach you. But as his anointing teaches you about all things and as that anointing is real, not counterfeit—just as it has taught you, remain in him."

The view that all roads lead to God is not true unless you remove words spoken by Christ like this: "I am the way, the truth, and the life: no man comes to the father, but by me." (John 14:6) There are just so many choices that are available and how does one know?

You must start with the Bible.

You must call out to God.

You must repent and accept Christ as your savior.

You must ask the Holy Spirit to lead you into all truth.

You must be prepared for change.

You must want the truth at any price.

You must understand your search, like mine, will become dangerous.

Are you willing to be different?

Can you overcome the prejudices and biases each of us inherited while growing up?

You must be willing to read both sides of all arguments.

Are you ready to read a book that might expose the untruth of the organization to which you belong?

Is finding the truth your ultimate goal?

Is finding God what you honestly want?

Is knowing where your eternity will be spent important?

WHAT DO I NEED TO DO?

God wants us to recognize that we need His help; that we are unable to pay for our wrongs. God wants us to accept His gift of salvation that He provided. This is Jesus who died on the cross for our wrongdoings. He was perfect and He went to the cross for each one of us. If I had been the only person ever born, he would still have done it. He did it for you, too. God wants us to call upon the name of Jesus to be saved. This simply means asking Christ to be our Savior and submitting our will to His. We place Him on the throne that was His to begin with. He will not force us.

Once we do this with a sincere heart, and God will know if it is real, just like you know, He will regenerate you as He has been doing to people for over two thousand years. This is done by faith. God's Holy Spirit will enter you, and reside with you, and from this day forward you will have the comforter of God with you always. God's Word says we are **"JOINT HEIRS WITH CHRIST."** This is a completely new relationship. Think about what this really means. Joint heirs with whom? Jesus, The Son of God!

HURDLES

Can someone have committed too many sins to be forgiven or a terrible single sin that haunts them even to this day? No, Jesus paid for ALL sin. He paid for the past, present, and future sins of ALL humankind ever.

I'm stuck in a serious sin. It really does not matter to God. It may matter to some church or religious people. However, your future is on the line, so who cares about what they think? God tells us to come as we are. He knows we are incapable of saving ourselves or fixing ourselves. He has a plan for that, also. It will not be your job. It now belongs to God and His Holy Spirit. Remember, this is about getting the ultimate Helper. It is a process called sanctification. You ask and the Holy Spirit begins to remove your chains of bondage.

Are there Christians in every denomination? Absolutely. As much as I dislike statistics, they do make a critical point. They state that approximately 14% of Catholics, 32% of Main Line denominations and 69% of Evangelicals are re-born. Every Christian denomination or church has those who are re-born and those who are not re-born. The percentage with each organization will vary based on many factors. Remember the Bondage Boys. They add to Scripture, which is a hindrance. The most important factor will depend on how clearly the Holy Scriptures are used to explain the truth as to what God has for each of us.

There you have it, **The GOOD NEWS!** – God is for you – God loves you – God has a plan for you – God forgives you – God will reconcile you - God will set you free – God forgets your sin – God is able to help you.

There is a catch: You need to repent.

(You admit you have been going the wrong way. You are asking forgiveness for your sins.)

CALL ON JESUS CHRIST

GOD GIVES SALVATION AS A GIFT

You can do this at any time. You need no one's approval or help. The Bible says, "TODAY is the day of your salvation. Tomorrow may not come." Why wait? It was the best decision I ever made. It means that you not only have understood what I have shared intellectually, but you have done what I was unable to do without God's intervention or push. You have decided to change, a heart change. This requires a simple, yet extremely difficult, acceptance that God has provided for us. It requires that you only do what God has required. It has nothing to do with being religious. It only has to do with responding to what God has revealed to us. It is not about pleasing men. It is simply about recognizing what the God of the universe has stated and has done for us. It is not about what others think. This is about securing a place in heaven. It is about your soul. It is about finding out that there is more to life than consumption. It is about seeing the big picture. God has more for each of us. God promises He will give us an abundant life down here with a real purpose and a reason. Have you ever wanted it to truly count?

Now, it will. What you do for God counts, and will forever. This is the time to make a bold move. Repent means to admit that you have sinned. Asking Christ to save you is to admit that you are willing to accept the only provision that God will accept. Wanting to have a new heart, perspective, as well as a helper inside you are benefits of making a right decision. Make this day the day you enter into the Kingdom. God tells us the angels rejoice as each of us surrender to the Truth.

An example:

I_____ repent of my sins. I know I fall short and miss the mark. I am thankful for the mercy of God. I am thankful that God loves me. I am thankful that someone cares enough that I have heard the truth. God forgive me. I accept Jesus as my personal savior. Please Jesus, come into my heart. May the Holy Spirit transform me into what you have planned. Thank you.

NOW YOU ARE READY FOR THE FINAL TRUMPET

OVERVIEW OF PROPHECY - MAJOR EVENTS

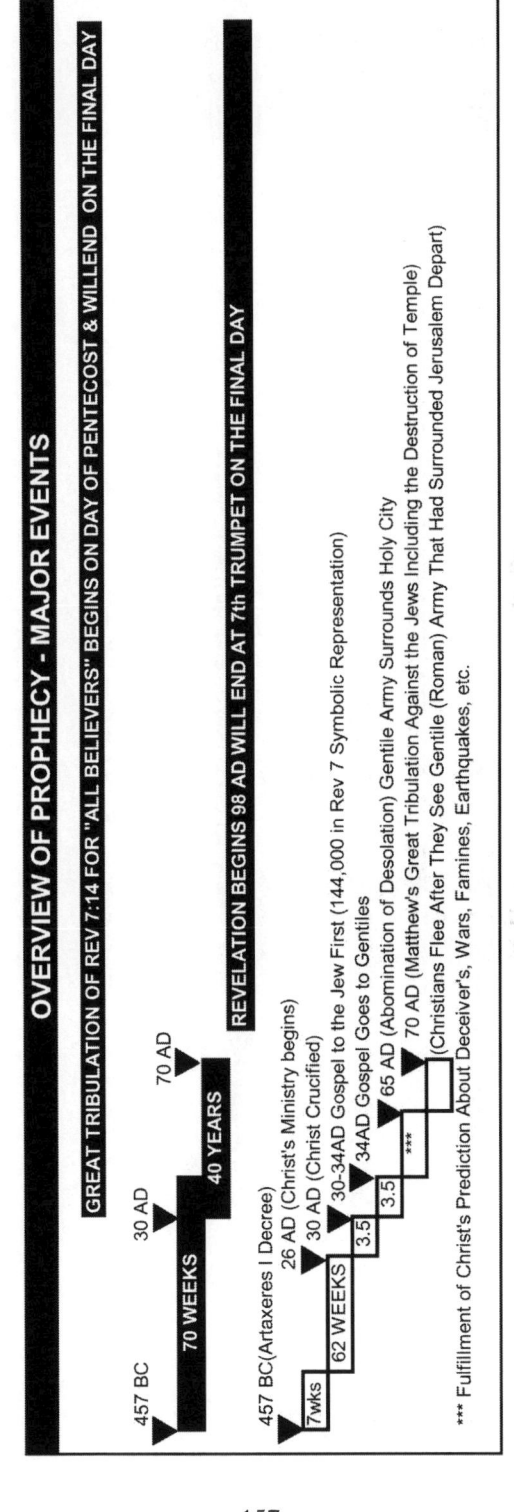

GREAT TRIBULATION OF REV 7:14 FOR "ALL BELIEVERS" BEGINS ON DAY OF PENTECOST & WILL END ON THE FINAL DAY

REVELATION BEGINS 98 AD WILL END AT 7th TRUMPET ON THE FINAL DAY

- 457 BC
- 30 AD
- 70 AD
- 70 WEEKS
- 40 YEARS

- 457 BC (Artaxeres I Decree)
- 26 AD (Christ's Ministry begins)
- 30 AD (Christ Crucified)
- 30-34AD Gospel to the Jew First (144,000 in Rev 7 Symbolic Representation)
- 34AD Gospel Goes to Gentiles
- 65 AD (Abomination of Desolation) Gentile Army Surrounds Holy City
- 70 AD (Matthew's Great Tribulation Against the Jews Including the Destruction of Temple)
- (Christians Flee After They See Gentile (Roman) Army That Had Surrounded Jerusalem Depart)
- 7wks
- 62 WEEKS
- 3.5
- 3.5

*** Fulfillment of Christ's Prediction About Deceiver's, Wars, Famines, Earthquakes, etc.

OVERVIEW OF MAJOR EVENTS IN REVELATION

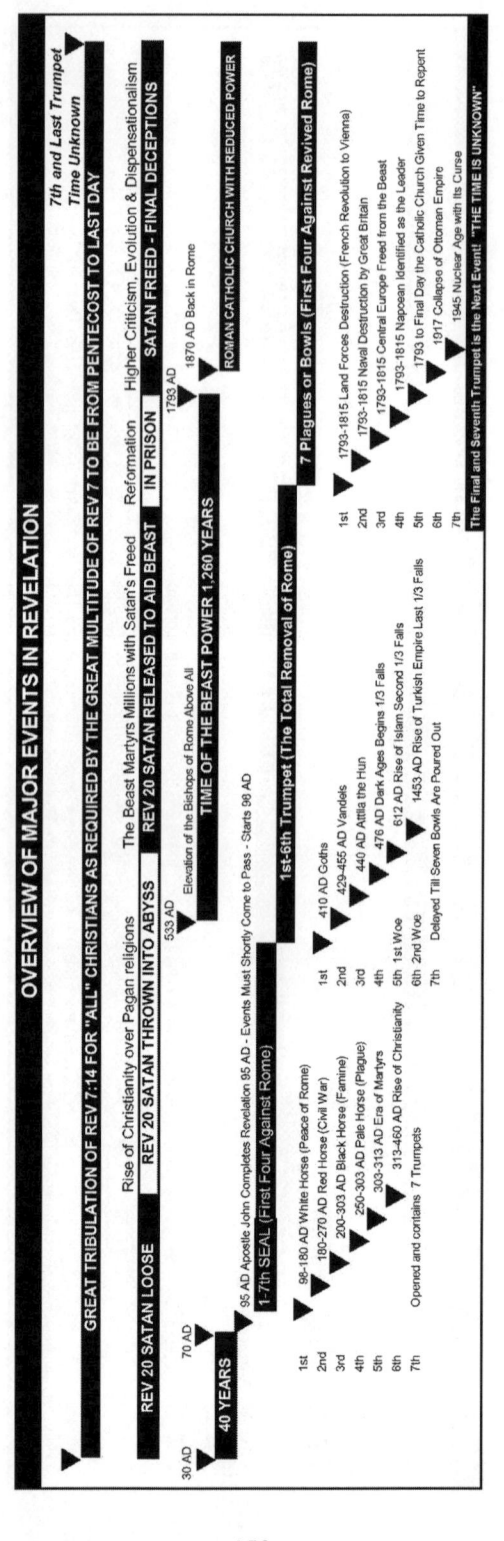

GREAT TRIBULATION OF REV 7:14 FOR "ALL" CHRISTIANS AS REQUIRED BY THE GREAT MULTITUDE OF REV 7 TO BE FROM PENTECOST TO LAST DAY

REV 20 SATAN LOOSE	Rise of Christianity over Pagan religions	The Beast Martyrs Millions with Satan's Freed Reformation	Higher Criticism, Evolution & Dispensationalism		7th and Last Trumpet Time Unknown
	REV 20 SATAN THROWN INTO ABYSS	REV 20 SATAN RELEASED TO AID BEAST	IN PRISON	SATAN FREED - FINAL DECEPTIONS	

30 AD
70 AD

40 YEARS

95 AD Apostle John Completes Revelation 95 AD - Events Must Shortly Come to Pass - Starts 96 AD

1-7th SEAL (First Four Against Rome)

- 1st: 96-180 AD White Horse (Peace of Rome)
- 2nd: 180-270 AD Red Horse (Civil War)
- 3rd: 200-303 AD Black Horse (Famine)
- 4th: 250-303 AD Pale Horse (Plague)
- 5th: 303-313 AD Era of Martyrs
- 6th: 313-460 AD Rise of Christianity
- 7th: Opened and contains 7 Trumpets

Elevation of the Bishops of Rome Above All
533 AD
TIME OF THE BEAST POWER 1,260 YEARS

1st-6th Trumpet (The Total Removal of Rome)

- 1st: 410 AD Goths
- 2nd: 429-455 AD Vandals
- 3rd: 440 AD Attila the Hun
- 4th: 476 AD Dark Ages Begins 1/3 Falls
- 5th 1st Woe: 612 AD Rise of Islam Second 1/3 Falls
- 6th 2nd Woe: 1453 AD Rise of Turkish Empire Last 1/3 Falls
- 7th: Delayed Till Seven Bowls Are Poured Out

1793 AD
1870 AD Back in Rome
ROMAN CATHOLIC CHURCH WITH REDUCED POWER

7 Plagues or Bowls (First Four Against Revived Rome)

- 1st: 1793-1815 Land Forces Destruction (French Revolution to Vienna)
- 2nd: 1793-1815 Naval Destruction by Great Britain
- 3rd: 1793-1815 Central Europe Freed from the Beast
- 4th: 1793-1815 Napoean Identified as the Leader
- 5th: 1793 to Final Day the Catholic Church Given Time to Repent
- 6th: 1917 Collapse of Ottoman Empire
- 7th: 1945 Nuclear Age with Its Curse

The Final and Seventh Trumpet is the Next Event "THE TIME IS UNKNOWN"

RECOMMEMDED READING

APOLOGETICS
McDowell, Josh, The New Evidence That Demands A Verdict, ISBN 0-7852-4219-8
Morison, Frank, Who Moved The Stone?, ISBN 0-310-29561-0
CHRISTIAN LIVING
Piper, John, Desiring God, ISBN 0-88070-869-7
CREATION BOOKS
Bird, W.R., The Origin Of Species Revisited, Vol. 1, ISBN 0-8407-6845-1
Bird, W.R., The Origin Of Species Revisited, Vol. 2, ISBN 0-8407-6848-6
Bullinger, E.W. Number In Scripture, 0-8254-2238-8
Gentry, Robert, V. Creation's Tiny Mystery, ISBN 0-9616753-3-0
Johnson, Phillip,E., Reason in the Balance, ISBN 0-8308-1610-0
Johnson, Phillip,E., Darwin On Trial, ISBN 0—8308-1324-1
Morris, Henry, M., The Long War Against God, ISBN 0-8010-6257-8
Morris, Henry, M., The Biblical Basis for Modern Science, ISBN 0-010-6178-4
Whitcomb, John, C. and Morris, Henry, M., The Genesis Flood, ISBN 0-87552-338-2
EDUCATION
Blumenfield, Samuel, NEA Trojan Horse in American Education, ISBN 0-941995-07-0
Morris, Barbara, M. Change Agents in the Schools, ISBN 0-931650-00-3
Schlafly, Phyllis, Child Abuse in the Classroom, ISNB 0-34640-10-6
ETHICS
Geisler, Norman, Christian Ethics, ISBN 0-8010-3832-4
Hughes, Philip, Christian Ethics in Secular Society, ISBN
GRACE
Yancy, Phillip, What's So Amazing About Grace?, ISBN 0-310-21327-4
HISTORY
Barton, David, Webster, Noah, Advice to the Young, ISBN 0-9295279-34-X
Barton, David, The Bulletproof George Washington, ISBN 0-9295279-14-5
Beliles, Mark, Thomas Jefferson's Abridgement of the Works of Jesus of Nazareth, No ISBN #
Berry, Grinton, Foxe's Book of Martyrs, ISBN 0-8010-3483-3
Bradford, M.E., Founding Fathers, ISBN 0-7006-0656-4, 0-7006-0657-2
Eidsmore, John, Columbus & Cortez, Conquers for Christ, ISBN 0-89221-223-3
LaHaye, Tim, Faith of Our Founding Fathers, ISBN 0-943497-00-0
Manuel, David, and Marshall, Peter, The Light and the Glory, ISBN 0-8007-0886-5 Cloth & 0-8007-5054-3 Paper

R. W. Mills

Manuel, David and Marshall, Peter, <u>From Sea to Shining Sea</u>, ISBN 0-8007-1451-2 Cloth & 0-8007-5308-9 Paper
Manuel, David and Marshall, Peter, <u>Sounding forth The Trumpet,</u> ISBN 0-8007-1746-5 Cloth
Millard, Catherine, <u>The Rewriting of America's History</u>, ISBN 0-88965-092-6

LAW ISSUES
Barton, David, America: <u>To Pray or Not To Pray</u>, ISBN 0-9295279
Barton, David, <u>The Myth of Separation</u>, ISBN0-9295279-06-4
Barton, David <u>Original Intent</u>, ISBN 0-925279-50-1
Buzzard, Lynn R., <u>Freedom and Faith</u>, ISBN 0-89107-230-6
Eidsmore, John, <u>Christianity and the Constitution</u>, ISBN 0-8010-3444-2
Hart, Benjamin, <u>Faith & Freedom</u>, ISBN 0-929510-00-3, 0-89840-239-5

NOT EXACTLY
Jones, Rick, <u>Understanding Roman Catholicism</u>, ISBN 0-937958-48-4
Martin, Walter, <u>The Kingdom of the Cults</u>, ISBN 1-55661-714-3
Matrisciana, Caryl and Oakland, Roger, <u>The Evolution Conspiracy</u>, ISBN 0-98981-939-4
Woodrow, Ralph, <u>Babylon Mystery Religion,</u> ISBN 0-916938-00-X

PROPHECY
Caringola, Robert, <u>Seventy Weeks The Historical Alternative</u>, ISBN 0-1-56043-445-7
Caringola, Robert, <u>The Present Reign of Jesus Christ,</u> ISBN0-9649189-0-0
Gasque, Ward, W., and Armerding, Carl, E. (Edited by), <u>Handbook of Biblical Prophecy,</u> ISBN 0-8010-0135-8
Gregg, Steve (Edited by), <u>Revelation Four Views A Parallel Commentary</u>, ISBN 0-8407-2128-5
Miller, Fred, p., <u>Revelation A Panorama Of The Gospel Age</u>, ISBN 1-883116-01-6
Payne, Barton, J., <u>Encyclopedia of Biblical Prophecy</u>, ISBN 0-8010-7051-1
Woodrow, Ralph, <u>Great Prophecies Of The Bible</u>, ISBN 0-916938-02-6
Woodrow, Ralph, <u>His Truth Is Marching On</u>, ISBN 0-916938-03-4
Examples of Dispensationalism
LeHaye, Tim, **No Fear of the Storm,** Why Christians Will Escape All The Tribulation, ISBN# 0-88070-514-0
Lindsey, Hal, <u>The 1980's: Countdown To Armageddon</u>, No ISBN #
Lindsey, Hal, <u>The Late Great Planet Earth</u>, No ISBN#
Example of Pretist
Gentry, Kenneth, <u>Before Jerusalem Fell</u>, ISBN: 0-915815-31-1

STATISTICS
Barna, George, <u>What Americans Believe</u>, ISBN 0-8307-1505-3

THEOLOGICAL ISSUES
Lewis, C.S., <u>The Problem Of Pain</u>, ISBN 0-02-06850-2
Yancy, Phillip, <u>Disappointment with God</u>, ISBN 0-310-51781-8
Yancy, Phillip, <u>Where Is God When It Hurts?</u>, ISBN 0-310-35411-0

17254328R00104

Printed in Great Britain
by Amazon